SCHOLASTI

Reteaching Math
ADDITION & SUBTRACTION

Mini-Lessons, Games & Activities to Review
& Reinforce Essential Math Concepts & Skills

Denise Birrer, Stephanie DiLorenzo & Bob Krech

New York • Toronto • London • Auckland • Sydney
Mexico City • New Delhi • Hong Kong • Buenos Aires

Teaching
Resources

DEDICATION

For Daniel and Kaya
—DB and SD

ACKNOWLEDGMENTS

We would like to thank Marilyn Hynes and Mary Ann Fornal for their constant support
and encouragement to take risks. It is a pleasure working with such wonderful professionals
and caring friends.
—DB and SD

Editor: Mela Ottaiano
Cover design by Brian LaRossa
Interior design by Holly Grundon
Interior illustrations by Mike Moran

ISBN-13: 978-0-439-52964-8
ISBN-10: 0-439-52964-6

Table of Contents

Table of Contents (continued)

REPRODUCIBLE STUDENT PAGES

Introduction

Most math books that have the word *reteaching* in the title typically feature many pages of equations and practice problems. The reasoning may be that if students require a concept or skill to be retaught, the best way for them to gain mastery is to practice more of the same. Research does show that some students need more time on a task than other students in order to learn a concept. However, if a student does not understand a concept or skill the first time, presenting a series of problems that the student already finds difficult and repeating them, without new knowledge or intervention, will most likely not be successful.

To reteach implies actually teaching again, not merely repeated practice. Students need to have a strong conceptual understanding if they are going to be able to do mathematics with accuracy and comprehension. Without this understanding, math can become meaningless and students simply work by rote. That's why we've created the Reteaching Math series. You will find this series is different from most reteaching books in that the emphasis is on helping students develop understanding as well as providing useful practice.

Teaching Tip

. . . .

Math Journal/Notebook

Have students keep their math notes, practice papers, and other work in a math journal/notebook. This can be a simple three-ring binder with some blank lined paper. Throughout this book you will find journal prompts that will help your students solidify their understanding of concepts by writing explanations about the ideas in their own words. As they do this, students will be creating their own personal math reference book. The practice pages, which include a Basics Box, should be kept in the journal as well so students will be able to refer back to previous work to help them with definitions, skills, concepts, and ideas.

Using a Problem-Solving Approach

The activities, games, and lessons in this book are just plain good instruction, with an emphasis on solving problems and applying math in context. Problem solving is the first process standard listed in the NCTM *Principles and Standards for School Mathematics* (2000). The accompanying statement reads, "Problem solving should be the central focus of all mathematics instruction and an integral part of all mathematical activity." In other words, problem solving is what math is all about. Every lesson here begins with a problem to solve to help create a spirit of inquiry and interest. Practice problems are integrated into the lessons so they are meaningful. Real reteaching!

Providing Context

It is important to provide students with a context to help give learning mathematical skills and concepts meaning. Context helps learners understand how these mathematical ideas and tools are useful and can be applied to real-life problems and situations. Context can be provided by creating a theme that carries throughout all the lessons. In this book, the theme of the Zoo Zone provides a context in which learning about addition and subtraction is relevant, motivating, and fun. The use of the overarching Zoo Zone theme gives all the lessons a sense of cohesion, purpose, and interest.

What's Inside?

Activity Lessons – introduce major concepts and skills. Timed to last about 40 minutes, these lessons are designed to help students work on the ideas in a hands-on manner and context to help them understand the meaning behind the math and give them an opportunity to apply it in a fun way.

Practice Pages – are specially designed to provide both practice and a helpful reference sheet for students. Each practice page begins with a word problem so students can see how and why the math is useful in solving real problems. Each page also features a **Basics Box**. Here, concepts are carefully presented with words, numbers, pictures, definitions, and step-by-step explanations. **Example problems** help solidify understanding, then a series of problems give students practice. Finally, a **journal prompt** helps students discuss and explore the concept using pictures, numbers, and words, while providing you an assessment opportunity that looks at student thinking and understanding. Practice pages can be worked on together in class, assigned to be done independently, or given as homework assignments.

Review Pages – provide students with additional focused practice on a specific math concept. The concept is practiced in a variety of formats and is designed to be completed independently. In addition, a **mixed review** of concepts introduced earlier is included in many review pages. By spiraling the curriculum in this way, students' retention and recall of math ideas is supported. These pages may be

Addressing Various Learning Styles

A good way to help all students learn mathematics well is to present ideas through physical, pictorial, and symbolic representations. Research suggests the importance of learning math ideas through modeling with manipulatives. Math concepts need to be experienced on a physical level before pictorial and more abstract representations can be truly understood. Relying completely on symbolic representations (e.g., lots of equations) is rarely enough, particularly in a reteaching situation.

Learning experiences featured here include using manipulatives, drawing pictures, writing equations, reading stories, and playing games to help learners gain a strong conceptual knowledge.

About Addition and Subtraction

Addition and subtraction are so much a part of our daily lives that we don't realize how often we use these ideas. Working with recipes, balancing checkbooks, shopping, and planning schedules are all real-life, everyday contexts in which we constantly add and subtract. Addition and subtraction are the basic operations on which more complex operations, like multiplication and division, are built.

A large part of working with addition and subtraction in the elementary grades has centered on memorization of the basic addition and subtraction facts. You will find that this is still very much a primary goal in this book, but that memorization is supported by addition and subtraction strategies and the development of a solid understanding of the underlying concepts.

The big idea with these two key operations is that quantities all around us are constantly changing, either with more being added on, or some being taken away. The quantities could be dollars, marbles, sugar, miles, or even time. To keep track of these changes we need a solid understanding of addition and subtraction.

How to Use This Book

This book can be used as a replacement unit, as a resource for activities for math workshops or centers, or as a supplement to find engaging ideas to enhance a textbook unit. The lessons and activities are presented in a developmental sequence, but can be used as stand-alone or supplementary learning experiences. Since it's written to accommodate all learners you can use it to teach a unit on addition and subtraction to any class.

Addition and subtraction are basic mathematical operations that students need to thoroughly understand before moving to more complex operations like multiplication and division. By using an active, engaging, problem-solving approach, you can help your students develop a solid foundation for future mathematical understanding and success.

Addition and subtraction are discussed in the NCTM Standards under the Numbers and Operations and Algebra Standards. The expectations for grades 2–4 include:

- understand various meanings of addition and subtraction of whole numbers and the relationship between two operations

- understand the effects of adding and subtracting whole numbers

- develop and use strategies for whole-number computations, with a focus on addition and subtraction

- develop a fluency with basic number combinations for addition and subtraction

- use a variety of methods and tools to compute, including objects, mental computation, estimation, paper and pencil, and calculators

- develop a fluency in adding, subtracting, multiplying, and dividing whole numbers

- develop and use strategies to estimate the results of whole-number computations and to judge the reasonableness of such results

- develop and use strategies to estimate computations involving fractions and decimals in situations relevant to students' experience

- use visual models, benchmarks, and equivalent forms to add and subtract commonly used fractions and decimals

- illustrate general principles and properties of operations, such as commutativity, using specific numbers

- model situations that involve the addition and subtraction of whole numbers, using objects, pictures, and symbols

- identify such properties as commutativity, associativity, and distributivity and use them to compute with whole numbers

Within these expectations are more specific objectives. These are addressed in the learning experiences throughout this book and include:

- recognize and use fact strategies for addition and subtraction

- add and subtract whole numbers

- use appropriate vocabulary for addition and subtraction

- solve basic and two- and three-digit addition and subtraction problems with and without regrouping

- develop a variety of methods (manipulatives, pictures, numbers, and words) to solve addition and subtraction problems and explain thinking

- solve story problems using addition and subtraction

Part 1: Addition

Materials

For each student:

- Letter #1 (p. 38)
- 25 counting manipulatives (e.g., chips, cubes)
- math journal/notebook
- pencil

Teaching Tip

The Imaginative Approach

Tapping into children's imaginations is a great way to get them excited about math. A fictitious company like the Zoo Zone provides a fun and engaging context for learning. Basing all the lessons around one main theme gives the students time to grow in their skills while feeling part of a larger task. This in turn motivates them to complete all lessons and reach the final goal. Students who are interested and excited by a task always learn more from the activities. Using an imaginative approach helps this happen.

ACTIVITY LESSON #1

The Zoo Zone Wants You

(INTRODUCING THE ZOO ZONE, ADDITION, AND RELATED VOCABULARY)

> Overview: This lesson introduces the Zoo Zone theme. Students also begin to think about and verbalize what they know about addition.

The letter introduced in this first lesson will help engage your students immediately as the fictitious Zoo Zone Company asks them to help with the opening of a new zoo.

Before class starts, place copies of Letter #1 in a large envelope addressed to the class. (Add a return address and postage if you'd like! For added fun, have a colleague deliver the envelope to your classroom).

Hold up the envelope and have students predict what might be inside. Open the envelope and say, "There are copies of a letter in here, and it looks like there are enough for each of us to have one. Let's pass them out so that we can all have a chance to read them."

Pass out the copies and give the class a few minutes to read the letter independently. Say, "This letter seems important, but there is a lot of information. Let's read and review it together." Invite students to take turns reading the letter aloud. Lead a discussion about the letter, making sure to clarify the ideas and define any unfamiliar vocabulary.

Point out the necessity of math, particularly addition and subtraction. Take the remainder of this lesson time to help students prepare individual math journals for the Zoo Zone tasks ahead.

ACTIVITY: What Is Addition?

Begin by reminding students that the letter from the Zoo Zone said that they would need to use addition and subtraction to complete jobs. Say, "Let's look at a task similar to what you might be doing for the Zoo Zone." Share the following problem:

> A Zoo Zone worker was feeding the rabbits yesterday and he gave them 11 carrots. An hour later, they were still hungry, so he fed them 7 more carrots. How many carrots should he report that he fed the rabbits? *(18 carrots)*

List student responses on the board or a chart, always asking questions such as "How do you know?" or "How did you figure that out?" If students reply, "By adding," ask, "What does 'adding' mean?" *(Adding involves the joining or combining of smaller groups to create a larger group or the combining of parts into one whole.)*

Have students return to their desks or a work area where manipulatives are set up for their use. Tell the students that you will share a second job with them to solve. They may use the manipulatives if they would like. Tell students that their job is not only to solve the problem, but also to explain how they solved it using words, pictures, and/or numbers in their journals and to be prepared to share these ideas. Read aloud the following story problem:

> At the Zoo Zone, 12 chimpanzees were playing in their habitat. The zoo workers were feeding the other 9 chimpanzees. How many chimpanzees does the Zoo Zone have in all?
> *(21 chimpanzees)*

Before the students set to work, as a class do one or more of the following:

- Have several students retell the story problem in their own words.

- Have students close their eyes and visualize the problem as you reread it; ask several students to describe the action they "saw."

Allow students about five minutes to work on solving the problem and explaining their thinking. Call students back to the meeting area with their journals and have several volunteers share their thinking and strategies. Ask students to prove that their answer is correct by showing their method. A good way to ask students to do this is by saying, "You told us what your answer is, but show us how this is true. Can you prove you are right?" Allow them to use manipulatives or pictures to do so.

Ask, "How did you know that you needed to add to solve this problem?" *(You were looking at the two smaller groups of chimpanzees and how they form a whole group. You needed to find out how many in all.)*

Finally, represent the problem with a number sentence (or revisit this if it was already represented by a student): 12 + 9 = 21 chimpanzees.

Teaching Tip

Analyzing Story/Word Problems

Analyzing story problems with your students helps them to clarify what information they are receiving and what math they need to do in order to solve the problem. It provides them with a method to approach any word problem they may encounter. By having students identify the facts, focus on the question, and use strategies as modeled above in this lesson, students will gain skills to help them successfully solve story problems independently.

Literature Link

Hershey's Kisses Addition Book
by Jerry Pallotta
(Scholastic, 2000)

This book introduces children to basic addition through the use of delicious Hershey's Kisses and some zany clowns! The clowns carry, drag, throw, and juggle them to illustrate addition equations. Most of the equations use single digits, but the book also goes into adding single digits to the number 10. Equations are presented horizontally and vertically, concentrating mostly on work with two addends. The final page is a subtraction equation, perfect as a lead-in to that related operation.

Materials

For each student:
• Altered Double Ten Frame (p. 39)
• Sums Exploration Chart (pp. 40 and 41)
• 100 Addition Facts Table (p. 42)
• 20 counters (e.g. chips, cubes)
• crayons or colored pencils

For teacher:
• Transparency of Altered Double Ten Frame
• 4 counters
• overhead markers

Examine and discuss these ideas:

• 12 and 9 as "addends," or the two numbers you are adding together to get the answer or total

• 21 as the "sum," or the answer to an addition problem

• the plus sign and equal sign

• writing the number sentence horizontally and vertically (how the _____ replaces the =)

• the idea that 9 + 12 will get you the same sum of 21 (turnaround partner/fact); it does not matter in which order you add the 2 smaller groups

To close the lesson or as a homework assignment, ask students to write one or two addition story problems involving zoo animals. Require students to provide the solutions as well. You can use these completed problems to compile a class book of "zoo addition problems," or use them as practice pages or homework as you move through the unit.

ACTIVITY LESSON #2

Building Basic Addition Facts
(OVERVIEW OF BASIC ADDITION FACTS)

Overview: Students physically build the 100 Basic Addition Facts they will be revisiting as they learn the basic addition strategies. By physically building the equations, learners are creating a foundation for understanding the facts they will be memorizing. (This activity will take two to three 40-minute periods to complete, but is very worthwhile.)

On the overhead, display the Altered Double Ten Frame sheet and 4 counters. Say, "Imagine we were at the Zoo Zone giving out balloons for the grand opening. These 4 counters will represent our balloons. If there were 2 people and we had to split up these 4 balloons among the 2 people, how many different ways could we do it? It wouldn't have to be a fair share, but it could be."

Invite answers and move counters to model the responses. Say, "I'm going to record these so I don't forget them." Write addition equations for each response modeled. You should find five ways and record them all. *(0 + 4, 4 + 0, 1 + 3, 3 + 1, and 2 + 2)*

Say, "For this sum of 4 balloons, we found five different ways it could be split up, five different ways to make the sum of 4."

Tell students, "You'll notice I recorded your ideas using equations or addition facts. It's easier than drawing pictures of the different arrangements. Today I am going to give you an exploration challenge to get you ready for your upcoming work with the Zoo Zone. I'm going to give you some sums and I want you to find all the possible addition facts that will make a certain sum. Let's look at how we will do this."

Model the procedure with these directions:

1. Place 2 counters on the Altered Double Ten Frame sheet.

2. Move them into the two frames in as many different ways as you can think of.

3. As you find an arrangement, write down the fact that describes it on your Sums Exploration Chart.

4. Find that same fact on your 100 Addition Facts Table and color it in.

5. After you have found all the facts that work for that sum, write the number of facts you found on your chart, in the "# of ways" column. (One thing to remember: We are only using single-digit addends.)

6. Keep going until you have completed your chart.

7. Do you notice any patterns on your Sums Exploration Chart or 100 Addition Facts Table? Write down what you notice.

Note: Students will find there is no way to make 19 using single-digit addends. Students should notice that the number of ways to make each sum is one more than the sum itself up through nine. (For example, there are 10 ways to make 9.) Using only single-digit addends, the number of ways to make sums from 10 to 18 decreases. Students should also notice that the ways to make each sum run on a diagonal on the 100 Addition Facts Table. Circulate as students work, making sure that they are following the procedures described above. Discuss patterns they find and check results together.

Teaching Tip

Addition Word Wall & Essential Addition Vocabulary

Certain vocabulary will naturally emerge as you talk about addition with your students. Charting the vocabulary reinforces student understanding and serves as a class reference that provides assistance when students are explaining their thinking. You may also want to require students to copy vocabulary from the chart into their math journals along with an example, using numbers and pictures, to show their understanding. Include terms such as the following:

addend
all together
and
equation
in all
in total
join
number sentence
plus
put together
sum

Materials

For each student:
- Primate Shipping Form (p. 43)
- a sheet of centimeter square graph paper
- crayons or colored pencils
- Practice Page #3 (p. 44)
- Review Page #3 (p. 45)
- pencil

For teacher:
- Transparencies of the Primate Shipping Form and centimeter square graph paper
- overhead markers

Literature Link

Two of Everything
by Lily Toy Hong (Whitman, 1993)

This picture book is great as a read-aloud to introduce or reinforce the idea of "doubles." In the story, Mr. and Mrs. Haktak find a magic pot that doubles everything that goes into it. As you read, each time items go into the pot, have your students calculate how many items will come out.

ACTIVITY LESSON #3

Primate Playmates
(DOUBLES STRATEGY FOR ADDITION)

> Overview: Students learn the "Doubles" strategy to help them become proficient with basic addition facts.

To become proficient with basic addition facts, students need to develop good addition strategies. Memorization alone is not always sufficient. Children can memorize a fact without real understanding just as they might memorize a song in a foreign language and not know its meaning. If students learn strategies, they have a "math tool box" that they can rely on to help recall facts they may forget.

This lesson focuses on the concept of "Doubles" and its use as an addition strategy. Students learn Doubles with relative ease and can use them to help with more difficult computation and "Near Doubles Facts," like 7 + 8, which have addends one apart.

Tell students, "I have been informed by the Zoo Zone that your first task as members of the Zoo Zone Planning Committee is to set up habitats for the primates being shipped to the zoo. There is one very important rule when planning for the number of primates in each habitat. Primates need a playmate or a buddy. They prefer spending time with a fellow primate of the same species, rather than being alone. You will need to make sure that each primate shipped to the zoo has a playmate." (Note: Primates are mammals that have increased flexibility and development of the hands and feet, a shortened snout, and higher intelligence, such as gorillas, monkeys, and apes.)

"I suggest we use the addition strategy of Doubles to complete this job." Pose the question, "What does it mean to double a number?" *(When the number you are adding is the same in each group or when you add the same number to itself, such as 7 + 7 = 14.)*

Ask, "So if 5 gorillas are being shipped to the zoo, how many gorillas in total will need to live in the gorilla habitat?" *(10)* "How can you use doubles to figure that out?" *(5 + 5 = 10)*

Explain, "Completing this job for the zoo will also help you to learn or review some addition facts. Once you know your 'doubles facts' you will know 10 of your 100 basic facts. Doubles can help you with learning other basic addition facts."

Pass out a Primate Shipment Form (p. 43) and a sheet of centimeter square graph paper to each student. Explain, "This form tells how many of each primate will be arriving at the zoo. You need to sketch out the habitats on the graph paper and show how many of each primate will be living there by shading a number of squares and writing an addition fact that matches."

Say, "Let's try an example together." Refer back to the 5 gorillas. Point out where they are listed on the order form. Continue, "You already told me that there will need to be 10 gorillas in total living in the habitat. This way each gorilla will have a playmate. You figured this out with the 'doubles fact' $5 + 5 = 10$."

Demonstrate this on the overhead copy of the centimeter square graph paper. Say, "I am using my red marker to shade in 5 squares to represent the 5 gorillas being shipped to the zoo. I am using my blue marker to shade in 5 squares to represent the 5 playmates. I am going to trace around the habitat with a black marker to show its boundaries. It has 10 squares in total, which stands for 10 gorillas. Underneath the habitat I will write my number sentence $5 + 5 = 10$ gorillas. I am making sure to put the label 'gorillas' so that the Zoo Zone Company knows that this is the gorilla habitat. Now, you need to do the same for all of the primates listed on your shipping form. You should do the gorillas again on your own plan."

Circulate to see that students are drawing their Doubles in two different colors on the graph paper and representing them with a number sentence. Review together when complete.

Teaching Tip

Addition Strategies Chart

As you introduce your students to addition strategies, create a Class Strategies Chart. The chart should name the strategy, provide an explanation and illustration, and include several examples of basic facts where the strategy would be useful. Having students help make the chart is extremely valuable. Keeping the chart as a reference in the classroom serves as a visual reminder to students to utilize their strategies. It will also help students verbalize the strategies they are using when explaining their thinking and reasoning.

ACTIVITY LESSON #4

Math Secrets

(*Introducing the Math Secrets Handbook*)

> **Overview:** Students begin to collect math strategies and reference sheets into a handbook. Students review the "Doubles" strategy for addition.

The Math Secrets Handbook is an ongoing component throughout the study of addition strategies. To introduce this idea, tell students, "Today you will begin making your own Math Secrets Handbook that will explain all the addition strategies we are learning about. You will be responsible for completing a Math Secret page after each addition strategy that we learn about, starting with 'Doubles.' Anyone who might need to learn addition strategies should be able to read your handbook and understand how to use these strategies.

Materials

For each student:
- Math Secret (p. 46)
- 100 Addition Facts Table (p. 42)
- pencil
- manila folder (to become the "Math Secrets Handbook")

Teaching Tip

The Meaning of Efficiency

Introduce your students to the word *efficient* when working on strategies. *Efficient* means doing something well and in a timely manner. Explain that mathematicians need tools just like carpenters do, to make their jobs easier and more efficient. Strategies are math tools. They help you do math quickly and correctly. There are some ways to add that are more efficient than others. For example, when solving an addition word problem, it is possible to use your fingers, and most students will, at first. However, numbers eventually get too big for fingers, and using fingers is a slow, sometimes inaccurate process. On the other hand, using memorized math facts to solve problems is efficient because it is both fast and accurate.

Literature Link

Anno's Magic Seeds
by Mitsumasa Anno
(Philomel, 1995)

This book is a more advanced look at Doubles, embedded in a wonderful Japanese tale. Children who like brainteasers will have fun working out the doubling problems. You may wish to use it as a small group read aloud for more capable students.

Say, "Turn and talk to a partner. Tell him or her what you know about 'Doubles' and how you might explain Doubles to the zoo workers." (*Doubles can be difficult to explain. A suggested explanation is: "Doubles means that you add a number to itself; you are making the number twice as big. Doubles facts are easy to learn and they become 'helpers' or 'anchors' for 'Near-doubles' and other facts as well."*)

Distribute a copy of the Math Secret sheet (p. 46) to each student. Draw the students' attention to the blank spaces at the top of the page. Have students place a "1" in the space following "#." In the next space, have students write in the word "Doubles" to indicate the strategy. Explain your expectations to the students. Say, "The top box is for your *picture* example of the strategy. For instance, if you were explaining the Doubles strategy, you might draw 4 eagles and 4 parrots for a total of 8 birds. The lines in the middle are for explaining the strategy with *words*. The bottom box should be used to list the *facts* this strategy helps with. For example, with Doubles you can list the facts starting with 0 + 0 and ending with the nines." Students should list five equation examples. You can challenge students to list more, write more, or include another picture example. (Note: Follow the procedure above for each strategy.)

Students will also use a 100 Addition Facts Chart to highlight the facts pertaining to each strategy. Have students complete these forms while you circulate and assist. When these are complete, give each student a manila folder. Explain that this is where they will keep all of the secrets and reference sheets they will be working on, beginning with this lesson. Have students label the folder Math Secrets Handbook. They should include their name and decorate as they wish.

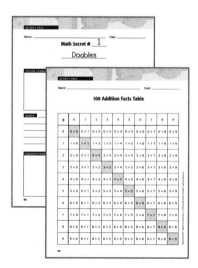

Have students complete these pages and add them to their handbook.

ACTIVITY LESSON #5

Playtime Pairing
(DOUBLES PLUS ONE STRATEGY FOR ADDITION)

Overview: Students learn and use the "Doubles Plus One" strategy for addition.

ACTIVITY: **Doubles Plus One Mini-Lesson**

Bring students together and review the concept of Doubles by listing all of the Doubles facts on the board or chart paper (see example below). Explain that students will be learning and using a new strategy called "Doubles Plus One" to complete a new assignment from the Zoo Zone. With the Doubles Plus One strategy, students will need to identify the smaller addend, double it, and add 1.

Next to the list of Doubles facts on the board or chart paper, write a list of related Doubles Plus One facts. Ask, "How does knowing these Doubles facts help you find the answer to these Doubles Plus One facts?" (*The facts are close to Doubles, they have addends that are only 1 apart. So, if you know the related Doubles fact, you just need to add one more to get the answer.*)

Doubles	Doubles Plus One
0 + 0	0 + 1
1 + 1	1 + 2
2 + 2	2 + 3
3 + 3	3 + 4
4 + 4	
5 + 5	
6 + 6	
7 + 7	
8 + 8	
9 + 9	

Demonstrate locating the smaller number and doubling it before adding 1 to create the Doubles Plus One equation. Ask for volunteers to solve the remaining facts using this new strategy.

Materials

For each student:
- Toy Order Form (p. 50)
- pencil
- Math Secret (p. 46)
- 100 Addition Facts Table (p. 42)
- Practice Page #5 (p. 51)
- Review Page #5 (p. 52)

For each pair of students:
- Playtime Pairing Directions, Game Board, and Animal Cards (pp. 47–49)

Teaching Tip

Fostering Number Sense Through Estimation

When solving math problems it is important for children to develop a sense of what answers are possible and logical. In other words, number sense. One way to help develop number sense is to have students get used to estimating before solving. In a problem like: *Ben was taking care of 12 chimps at the zoo. Then he got 7 more. How many chimps does Ben need to care for in all?* Children benefit from answering questions such as: Would the answer be more or less than 12? Would the answer be less than 20? Children who have a well-developed number sense truly understand the math behind the problem and are therefore able to determine if the math that they are doing "makes sense."

Following the activities, have students complete these pages for the Doubles Plus One Strategy and add them to their handbook. (See the procedure detailed on p. 14)

Materials

For each student:
- math journal/notebook
- pencil
- Petting Zoo Inventory (p. 53)
- Petting Zoo Pens (p. 54)
- crayons, colored pencils, or stamp pads
- Math Secret (p. 46)
- 100 Addition Facts Table (p. 42)
- Practice Page #6 (p. 55)
- Review Page #6 (p. 56)

For each pair of students:
- 10 two-color counters (or 20 counters, 10 of one color and 10 of another)

ACTIVITY: **"Playtime Pairing" Card Game**

Students will play a card game to help them practice the Doubles Plus One strategy.

Pair students and distribute a game board, directions sheet, and set of animal cards to each group. Read the rules and objectives of the game with the students.

In this game, students take turns choosing an animal game card from the pile. They will need to count the number of animals on the card and tell their partner the Doubles fact for that number. Example: If there are 4 elephants on the card, the student says that 4 + 4 = 8.

Next, the student pairs the animal card to the related "Doubles Plus One" fact on the game board. Example: With the elephants, the related "Doubles Plus One" fact is 4 + 5 = 9 / 5 + 4 = 9.

By matching the card to the related fact on the board, students will reveal which toy will need to be ordered for that animal's habitat. Once all of the animal cards are placed on the game board, both students will be responsible for recording the game results on a Toy Order Form (p. 50) for the Zoo Zone. On this form, the students will be given a list of the animals, and they will need to record the numbers and types of toys necessary for each animal's habitats.

ACTIVITY LESSON #6

Petting Zoo Placement
(MAKE TEN STRATEGY FOR ADDITION)

Overview: Students learn and use the "Make Ten" strategy for addition.

ACTIVITY: **Combinations of Ten**

This activity is a hands-on exploration of ways to make ten. By using manipulatives, the students will see visual representations of the combinations of ten, as they record them numerically.

Tell students, "Make Ten is an addition strategy that will help us in our next task from the Zoo Zone. Learning how to make and look for combinations of 10 is very useful in addition."

Explain, "We are going to use two-color counters to explore all the ways to make ten today." Pose the question, "If I was going to put my 10 counters into 2 groups, what is one way I could do that?" (*Possible suggestions: 2 and 8, 5 and 5, etc.*) Take one suggestion and confirm it by saying, "Yes, I could put 2 counters in one group and 8 counters in another group; 2 and 8 make 10." Demonstrate this as you speak, by putting 2 counters of one color in a group and 8 counters of the other color in a second group. Push the counters together to show how combining the 2 and the 8 makes 10 in all.

Distribute math journals/notebooks and 10 two-color counters to each pair. Explain the next task, "Working with partners, I would like you to explore all the possible ways to put your 10 counters into 2 groups. Both partners should make a list in your math journals of all the combinations you discover."

When pairs have finished, ask students to share their combinations for 10. List students' ideas on the board until all possible combinations have been given. (*0 + 10, 1 + 9, 2 + 8, 3 + 7, 4 + 6, 5 + 5, 6 + 4, 7 + 3, 8 + 2, 9 + 1, 10 + 0*) For an added challenge, ask students to generate a list of combinations using three addends to make 10.

ACTIVITY: **Petting Zoo Placement**

Say, "Now that you know about making combinations of 10, you are ready for your next assignment from the Zoo Zone. The Zoo Zone has sent an inventory sheet that lists the animals and how many there are of each. They have also sent you a form to organize the pens. Let's take a look at both together."

Tell students, "You will need to place animals in a petting zoo for children. The animals will be living in pens, where people can enter to pet and feed them. The Zoo Zone has found that it is best not to put more than 10 animals in one pen."

Look at the inventory sheet with the students, reading over the directions. Draw students' attention to the fact that they need to record their plan for the petting zoo placement on the form from the Zoo Zone. This is a great opportunity to introduce the concept of Ten Frames as organizational tools for math. Look at Petting Zoo Pens together. Point out how the pens are organized as Ten Frames, and when all the squares are full, you know you have 10 without even having to count.

Students should work independently or in pairs to plan the placement of the animals for the petting zoo, and represent where they will place each animal through a picture/symbol and a number sentence. You may want to have some students use multilink cubes of varying colors to represent the animals. For example, students may use red cubes to represent sheep and blue cubes to represent ponies,

Teaching Tip

·····································

Two-Color Counters

Two-color counters are an ideal manipulative for exploring combinations of 10. Students can see the combinations more clearly when using two different colors to represent the 2 different addends. If you do not own a class set of two-color counters, they are inexpensive and easy to make. Take a bag of dried lima beans, lay the beans out on newspaper, and spray paint one side. Allow to dry, then store in plastic bags or containers.

Teaching Tip

·····································

The Ten Frame as a Math Tool

The Ten Frame (see the Petting Zoo Pens, p. 54) is an excellent organizational tool when working with counting, addition, subtraction, and place-value concepts. A Ten Frame is a simple rectangle divided evenly into 10 sections. When all sections are full, you know you have 10 without needing to count in any way. Also, with 2 empty spaces in a Ten Frame, it is clear at a glance that there are 8 items. All facts with two addends are easily represented on Ten Frames.

Teaching Tip

Ten Frame Work Using Kid Pix

This activity can also be done using computers and any version of the kid-friendly software Kid Pix (Broderbund, Inc. 2000). Students could make the "Ten Frame Pens" themselves, using the rectangle and line tools, or you could prepare a template ahead of time. The stamp sets can be used to "stamp" the animals into their spots in the pens. By using the typewriter tool or number stamps, students can create accompanying number sentences.

Materials

For each student:

• 20 two-color counters

• Special Additions Work Mat, Game Cards, and Recording Sheet (pp. 57–59)

• pencil

• Math Secret (p. 46)

• 100 Addition Facts Table (p. 42)

• Practice Page #7 (p. 60)

• Review Page #7 (p. 61)

For teacher:

• Transparencies of the Special Additions Work Mat and Recording Sheet

• 13 two-color counters

• overhead markers

placing 6 red cubes and 4 blue cubes in a pen. Students can then color the squares red and blue to show where the cubes were placed and write a number sentence below the pen. *(6 sheep + 4 ponies = 10 animals)*

Another fun option is to have students use a stamp pad and make thumbprints to represent the animals. Once the ink dries, students can draw animal features on their thumbprints to make them look like animals.

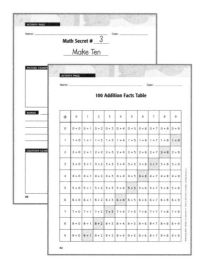

Following the activities, have students complete these pages for the Make Ten Strategy and add them to their handbook. (See the procedure detailed on p. 14)

ACTIVITY LESSON #7

Special Additions

(Special Nines Strategy for Addition)

> **Overview:** Students learn and use the "Special Nines" strategy for addition.

With basic facts that have nine as one of the addends, students can use the "Special Nines" strategy. There are two ways to approach this strategy. The first is visualizing the "nines problems" on a Ten Frame. Nine is so close to 10 that some students find it helpful to "pretend" that the 9 is a 10. For example with 9 + 4, imagine 9 red counters in a Ten Frame and 4 yellow outside of it. Then fill the

Ten Frame with a yellow counter to make ten. Since the one yellow counter comes from the 4 you are adding, there will be 3 more yellow counters left over. So, 9 + 4 is like 10 + 3 (13).

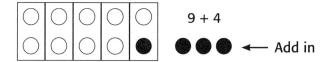

9 + 4   ← Add in

ACTIVITY: **Special Nines Mini-Lesson**

Bring students together and list all the nines facts on the board. Ask, "What do all of these facts have in common?" (*They all have a nine as one of the addends.*)

Explain, "Nines facts are easy because 9 is so close to 10. It is only 1 away. So, you can pretend that the 9 is a 10 to make your addition easier." Show students the following story problem:

> Paco earned 9 prize tickets at the carnival by hitting the target at the darts game. He earned 4 more prize tickets by making some baskets at the basketball game. How many tickets did Paco earn by playing both games?

Analyze the problem together. Once you have determined that it is necessary to add 9 + 4 to solve this problem, draw the students' attention back to the fact that one of the addends is a 9. Explain that you are going to demonstrate how to use the Special Nines strategy of visualizing the 9 as a 10. (Use the overhead copy of the Special Nines Work Mat, focusing on the portion with the two Ten Frames.) Display nine red (or same-colored) counters on a Ten Frame. Say, "There are 9 counters on my Ten Frame. Let's add 4 more. We are making the fact 9 + 4." Make sure that the 4 counters you are adding are yellow (or a color not used for the original nine).

Continue, "One of the 4 fits on the Ten Frame and fills it up." Place a yellow counter in the last square of the Ten Frame. "This makes 10. Three of the 4 are left over." Place the remaining 3 yellow counters in a second Ten Frame.

Explain, "Ten and 3 more is 13. So, 9 + 4 = 13. For Nines Facts, picture filling up the Ten Frame, then seeing how many are left over." Do several more examples with the class, having one student manipulate or draw the counters while another records the math with numbers.

Literature Link

· ·

Anno's Counting House
by Mitsumasa Anno
(Penguin, 1982)

In this picture book, ten children move from their old house into a new house. Throughout the pages, some of the children are covered while others are visible through cutout windows. Since only some of the ten children are visible through the windows, there are many opportunities for discussing "the other part of ten" that is missing.

Teaching Tip

Special Nines Trick

As you work with nines facts, some students may notice the "Special Nines Trick." Help students to verbalize that with nines facts, the ones digit in the sum is always one less than the number added to the nine. This is because one from that addend was "given" to the nine to make ten. (9 + 3 = 12; 9 + 4 = 13; 9 + 5 = 14) For some students this "trick" will be helpful in recalling these facts, while for other students, visualizing the problem on a Ten Frame is easier.

ACTIVITY: **Special Additions**

Say, "Many of the mother birds at the zoo are waiting for their eggs to hatch. New baby birds will be coming soon and the Zoo Zone needs to increase its supplies for the "new additions.""

Continue, "When the Zoo Zone opened its bird sanctuary, there were 9 adults of each species. Your job today will be to figure out how many of each species there will be once the babies hatch."

Suggest, "Since you will be adding the number of babies to the 9 adults, this would be a great opportunity to use 'Special Nines.'" Distribute the recording sheets, game cards, work mats, and counters to the students. Review the directions on the recording sheet together. Model for the students how to use the game cards and work mat to solve the addition facts by doing one example. Randomly choose a card from the pile. Place it on the work mat in the space provided. Use red counters to show the 9 adults on the top Ten Frame. Then use different-colored counters to represent the babies being added. Be sure to fill the top Ten Frame with the first "baby," then continue on to fill the bottom Ten Frame with the "leftover babies." Explain the math you are doing as you work. *(For example: 9 + 3 is being visualized as 10 and 2 left over to make 12.)*

After completing the math, demonstrate how to record the total on the Special Additions Recording Sheet. Find the bird species on the chart that matches the card. Write the equation and the total in the second column.

Have students work on completing the activity as you circulate and observe. Make sure that students are physically doing the math with the counters and Ten Frames before recording the totals on the sheet.

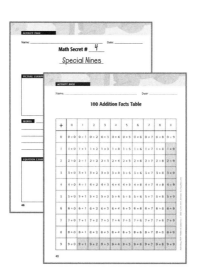

Following the activities, have students complete these pages for the Special Nines Strategy and add them to their handbook. (See the procedure detailed on p. 14)

Materials

For each student:
- Harmonious Habitats Recording Sheet (p. 62)
- pencil
- Math Secret (p. 46)
- Practice Page #7 (p. 63)
- Review Page #7 (p. 64)

For each pair of students:
- a pair of dice and a set of 12 multilink cubes
- a set of number cards (1–9)

ACTIVITY LESSON #8

Harmonious Habitats

(ADDITION STRATEGY: TURNAROUND PARTNERS)

Overview: Students learn that in addition, the order of the addends can be switched without changing the total. This idea is known as the commutative property or "Turnaround Partners."

ACTIVITY: **Turnaround Partner Roll and Build Game**

Begin this lesson by sharing the following story problem:

> Jamal had 7 marbles in his desk and 5 marbles in his backpack. Toni had 5 marbles in her desk and 7 marbles in her backpack. Stacey says Jamal and Toni have the same amount of marbles. Is that true? How do you know? (*It is true. You know because 7 + 5 has the same sum as 5 + 7, which is 12.*)

Work through the problem as a group. Use manipulatives to prove that both Jamal and Toni do indeed have the same total number of marbles. Write the equations to represent both Jamal's and Toni's marbles (7 + 5 = 12 and 5 + 7 = 12). Discuss the idea that in addition, you can switch the position of the addends without changing the total. These paired facts are called "turnaround partners." Ask students for other examples of turnaround partners.

Explain to students that they will be playing a game to get some practice with turnaround partners. Pass out a pair of dice, 12 multilink cubes, and journals for recording results to each pair of students. One player will roll a die and build the number shown using multilink cubes. The second player will roll the second die and build the number shown. Each partner will record the turnaround partner equations possible after joining the multilink cube trains and turning them around. Say, "See how many different turnaround partners you can make this way in the next five minutes." Share the results together as a class.

ACTIVITY: **Harmonious Habitats**

Say, "Now that we've done some turnaround partners practice, you are ready for your next Zoo Zone assignment. The Zoo Zone would like your help to determine how to fill some habitats with animals. A habitat is an area or environment where an animal lives. The Zoo Zone has included instructions and listed the habitats and their animals on

Following the activities, have students complete this page for the Turnaround Partners Strategy and add it to their handbook. (See the procedure detailed on p. 14)

Materials

For each student:

• math journal/notebook

• 3 counters

• Shopping List (p. 65)

• pencil

• Math Secret (p. 46)

• 2 copies of the 100 Addition Facts Table (p. 42)

• Practice Page #9 (p. 66)

• Review Page #9 (p. 67)

the recording sheet. You will be using your number cards to determine the possible animal number combinations."

Distribute and look at the Harmonious Habitats Recording Sheet. Model and practice with the first habitat, the arctic. Say, "In the first example on this sheet, you will need to determine the combinations of how many polar bears and walruses could be housed in this arctic habitat. Begin by selecting two number cards. Watch as I do it. For example, if you draw a 2 and a 5, you could have 2 polar bears and 5 walruses or 5 polar bears and 2 walruses in this arctic habitat. On my sheet I need to record these Turnaround Partners in the equation section. (Demonstrate as you say "2 polar bears + 5 walruses = 7 animals, just as 5 polar bears + 2 walruses = 7 animals.") Before the next player draws his or her cards, be sure to place the cards you have already used in a discard pile. Now it's your turn. Remember that both partners need to complete a Harmonious Habitats Recording Sheet.

. . . .

ACTIVITY LESSON #9

Counting On a Good Meal
(Counting On Strategy and Zero Strategy for Addition)

> **Overview:** Students practice both "Counting On," a helpful strategy when adding 1, 2, or 3 to a larger number, and "Zero Strategy."

Activity: **"Counting On" Mini-Lesson**

Say, "Today we will learn one final addition strategy. It is called "Counting On." This strategy is only useful when you are adding 1, 2, or 3 to a larger number. Otherwise, it really isn't the most efficient way to add, so be careful not to overuse it. Let's look at an example where Counting On would be helpful." Share this problem:

> Austin got 5 monkey stickers from his teacher and 2 giraffe stickers from his best friend. How many new stickers did Austin get in all?

Analyze the story problem with your students. Once it is determined that you will be adding 5 + 2 to find out how many new stickers Austin got in all, say, "Since 2 is one of the addends, we could use Counting On to help us if we didn't know what 5 + 2 was automatically. Let's try it."

Continue, "With Counting On, you always start with the bigger number, then count on. The bigger number is 5, so I will circle it. Can someone count on 2 more for us to get the answer?" Be sure to emphasize that 5 is *not* being counted; it is the starting point. Say, "So Austin got 7 new stickers in all." To help students use this strategy, suggest visualizing a number line and "hopping forward" or picturing the larger number and a set of 1, 2, or 3 dots to add on.

Reverse the addition one time with your students to help prove the efficiency of starting with the larger number when using this strategy. Say, "Let's look for a minute at why it is more efficient to start with the larger number and count on. What if we solved this same problem by adding the 5 monkey stickers to the 2 giraffe stickers?" Have a student use 2 as the starting point and count on 5 more to get to 7. Ask, "Is it easier or harder? Why?" (*It is harder. It takes longer. It can get confusing when you have to count on more than 1, 2, or 3. You lose your place.*)

Next do some oral Counting On practice with a variety of numbers. For example, "Let's start at 9; what would be 3 more? (*12*) Let's start at 27; what would be 2 more? (*29*)"

List 5 more facts on the board, some where Counting On would be efficient and some where it would not. (Also see the Teaching Tip on this page for a discussion of Zero Strategy.) Have students identify which facts would be appropriate for the Count On strategy. Have them verbalize the process as they solve them. You may want to throw in a few larger number examples here in order to show students how this strategy can be used with more difficult addition (Example: 27 + 3 or 423 + 2).

ACTIVITY: **Counting On a Good Meal**

Distribute math journals, 3 counters, and a copy of the Shopping List (p. 65) to each student. Tell students, "The next assignment for the Zoo Zone has arrived. Let's take a look at it." (Have students read the Shopping List silently, then read it aloud together.) Explain further, "The Zoo Zone is quite large, so it has two kitchens. Both kitchens are running low on certain foods and need to order more. This is a list from both kitchens. You need to add the amounts together for the workers so that they only need to place one order. I noticed that the main kitchen needs a larger amount of each food while the second kitchen needs much less. What strategy would work in this case?" (*Counting On*)

Look over the directions and the list with the students. Ask questions to ensure that students understand the task. "Who can tell me in their own words what the Zoo Zone workers are asking us to do?" (*Add up how much of each food they need to order*) "How will we get that total for each food?" (*By adding how much the second kitchen needs to how much the main kitchen needs*) "Why is the Counting On strategy useful here?" (*Because we are adding 1, 2, or 3 to a larger number*)

Teaching Tip

Zero Strategy

Make sure during the oral Counting On practice that at least one of the facts has zero as an addend (e.g., 9 + 0). When discussing these facts, be sure to stress that they are 'zero facts' and therefore there is no need to count on. When using the Zero Strategy the sum always equals the addend that isn't zero.

Teaching Tip

Strategies Summary

Counting On and Zero Strategy are the final addition strategies. After students complete the Counting On and Zero Strategy pages, they should assemble their handbooks. This can be done by stapling the pages into the right side of the manila folder, or by punching holes in each page and securing them with a brass fastener.

Then, using a pack of addition flash cards, review all of the addition strategies. Pick a strategy to practice and pull out those cards. Mix in an equal number of other cards. Show the cards one at a time to students. Ask a student to name the strategy and then give the answer. This may seem to slow down the recall process at first, but it is a very effective way to keep strategies fresh and useful to students.

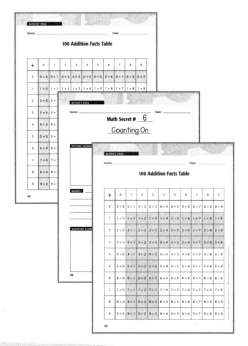

Tell the students that you would like them to complete their work in their journals. This will give them an opportunity to practice the Counting On strategy and demonstrate that they understand how to use it. At the same time, they will be accomplishing their task for the Zoo Zone.

Model how to show the addition for this task using an overhead, chart paper, or the board. (See the example below.) Do the first example for carrots together. Say, "Here is how I'd like you to show your math thinking today. First, I am going to write *carrots* on my paper as a label before I begin the math. Then I will draw a square around it. For carrots, the main kitchen needs 8 pounds and the second kitchen needs 2 pounds. If I was going to use the Counting On strategy to do this addition, which addend would I begin with?" (*8, because it is the larger number*)

Demonstrate how to use the counters to count on the 2 pounds. Place 2 counters next to the 8 card and count "9, 10" while touching each one. Draw 2 circles where the counters used to be and write a 9 and a 10 inside or underneath. Finish with an equal sign and the total (= 10 pounds).

$$\text{carrots} \quad \boxed{8} + \textcircled{9} \; \textcircled{10} = 10 \text{ pounds}$$

Students may notice that this is also a Make Ten fact. If they do not, draw their attention to it. This is a good example of how some facts can be solved using a variety of strategies.

Instruct students to complete the rest of the addition on their own, using the procedure you modeled. Circulate to make sure that they are physically completing the counting on and showing an understanding of the concept.

At the end of the activity, gather as a class to make a master list for the Zoo Zone workers. Students should bring their journals to the meeting area in order to check their work and contribute to the discussion. On the master list, simply list the food and the total amount to order.

Following the activities, have students complete these pages for the Counting On Strategy and Zero Strategy and add them to their handbook. (See the procedure detailed on p. 14 and the Teaching Tip above for more information.)

ACTIVITY LESSON #10

Animal Addends

(ADDING MULTIPLE ADDENDS)

> **Overview:** Having learned strategies for addition, students apply this knowledge to add more than two addends in a problem.

Materials

For each student:
- Animal Addends (p. 68)
- Practice Page #10 (p. 69)
- Review Page #10 (p. 70)
- pencil

Begin by sharing the following problem and asking students to solve it:

> The vet at the Zoo Zone needs to give a check-up to several animals. He needs to see 6 elephants, 2 rhinos, and 4 hippos. How many of the animals will the vet be checking on today?

Have students share responses. Guide the discussion by asking the following: "How did you arrive at your answer? Did you use any addition strategies? Is that the best strategy for helping us solve the problem with these particular number combinations? Did you use more than one strategy?" (Suggest that for this example, a good strategy is to first make 10 by adding 6 elephants and 4 hippos. After that, the 2 rhinos can be added on easily. Although students may try many strategies, it is important to suggest looking for Doubles and ways to Make Ten first, when examining multiple addends.)

Say, "In order to complete today's Zoo Zone job, you will need to not only solve addition problems with more than two addends, but you will need to tell what addition strategy or strategies you used in order to find the answer." Pass out an Animal Addends problem sheet (p. 68) to each student. Have students work independently and then compare results together. Note that the first problem is exactly the same as the example problem just completed as a class.

Part 2: Subtraction

Materials

For each student:
- Letter #11 (p. 71)

For each group of 3–5 students:
- a set of 20 manipulatives (multilink cubes, color tiles, counters)
- math journals/notebooks
- pencils

Literature Link

The Hershey's Kisses Subtraction Book
by Jerry Pallotta
(Scholastic, 2002)

This fun book teaches basic subtraction with the use of yummy Hershey's Kisses. It is a follow-up to the *Hershey's Kisses Addition Book*, and it features the same math-loving clowns and many good pictorial models. This book is a great, easy introduction to subtraction.

ACTIVITY LESSON #11

What Is Subtraction?

(*Introducing the Second Zoo Zone Letter, Subtraction Concepts, and Related Vocabulary*)

> **Overview:** Students begin to think about and verbalize their understanding of subtraction.

The next group of lessons focuses on basic subtraction concepts and fact strategies. Before starting the lessons in Part 2, distribute the second letter from the Zoo Zone to students in the suggested way described in Activity Lesson #1 (p. 8). Then, bring students together and share the following word problem:

> The zoo keeper was playing ball with 13 sea lions. 7 sea lions got tired and swam away. How many sea lions were left playing ball?

Ask students to solve the problem and share solutions. (*6 sea lions*) Analyze the problem, and have students explain their thinking. If a student says, "I solved it by subtracting," ask, "What does subtracting mean? What did you do to actually get the answer?" You may want to invite students to take five minutes at this point and use pictures, words, and number examples in their journals to explain their understanding of subtraction.

In discussion, be sure to draw attention to the idea that we started with a whole group and took one part away. In the end we were left with the other part of the group.

Say, "Now let's look at another story problem that uses subtraction in a different way." Show the students the following problem:

> Michael the monkey has 10 bananas. Missy the monkey has 6 bananas. How many fewer bananas does Missy have than Michael?

Say, "In this problem we are comparing two groups and looking at the difference. Let's draw Michael's bananas in one group and Missy's in another." Have student volunteers do this on the board. Continue,

"We can match up the number of bananas they have in common. The difference is what is left over. We are taking Missy's 6 bananas away from Michael's in order to find the difference." Finally, represent this by writing a subtraction equation. (10 – 4 = 6)

Tell students that you will show them two more story problems you would like them to solve in their journals. Provide manipulatives to those who want them. Remind students to show their work using words, pictures, and/or numbers.

Write these problems on the board and read together:

1. The Zoo Zone gift shop ordered 16 Zoo Book Magazines. There were 7 sold at the zoo's grand opening. How many magazines are left in the gift shop?

2. The Zoo Zone gift shop ordered 15 monkey stamps and 8 zebra stamps. How many more monkey stamps did they order than zebra stamps?

Explain to students that will have ten minutes to work on these two problems.

Afterward, have several volunteers share their thinking and strategies. When reviewing solutions, make sure to model the problems with manipulatives and pictures in order to physically show the separating of a larger group into two smaller parts or to show the difference between two groups. Finally, represent the problems with number sentences (or revisit this if it was already represented by a student).

Discuss these ideas:

- the "difference" is the answer to a subtraction problem

- the minus sign and equal sign

- writing the number sentence horizontally and vertically (how the _____ replaces the =)

- the idea that 16 – 7 = 9 and 16 – 9 = 7 are related, and made up of the same whole number and parts taken away

To close the lesson, or as a homework assignment, ask students to write one or two subtraction story problems involving zoo animals along with the solutions. These student-created word problems can be compiled in a class book of "Zoo Subtraction Problems," or used on practices pages or as homework as you move through the unit.

Literature Link

Elevator Magic
by Stuart J. Murphy
(HarperCollins, 1997).

This Mathstart series book explains subtraction through a rhyming text about a descending elevator. The main character, Ben, rides the elevator down from the tenth floor to the lobby. As it descends, it makes several stops, causing the subtraction (and magic) to start. Ben needs to subtract the number of floors he is traveling down in order to determine which button to push on the elevator panel. The book concludes with several easy-to-do extension activities.

Teaching Tip

Essential Subtraction Vocabulary

minus
take away
difference
how many more/fewer (comparing)
left
number sentence/equation
separate
related facts

Materials

For each student:
- math journal/notebook
- pencil
- Zoo Stamps (p. 72)
- scissors
- glue stick
- Practice Page #12 (p. 73)
- Review Page #12 (p. 74)

For teacher:
- Copy of Zoo Stamps
- colored markers

Teaching Tip

Subtraction Word Wall and Strategies Chart

As you did with addition strategies, you may want to keep a vocabulary chart and strategies chart for subtraction. Certain vocabulary will emerge, such as "the difference" and "minus" as you talk about subtraction with the students. By charting the vocabulary and the strategies (with examples) as you introduce them, it will reinforce understanding and provide assistance when students are explaining their thinking in writing or orally. You may also want to require students to copy vocabulary and strategies from the chart into their math journals along with an example using numbers and pictures.

ACTIVITY LESSON #12

Zoo Stamps Sale

(SUBTRACTION STRATEGY: COUNTING BACK)

Overview: Students practice "Counting Back," a helpful strategy when subtracting 1, 2, or 3 from a larger number.

ACTIVITY: **"Counting Back" Mini-Lesson**

Begin by reminding students of the Counting On addition strategy. Let them know that there is a similar strategy for subtraction called Counting Back. Then share this problem with students:

> Faith took a trip to the beach. She had 12 seashells in her backpack. She accidentally dropped the backpack and 3 seashells broke. How many seashells were still safely in one piece?

Analyze the problem with your students. Once it is determined that it is necessary to subtract the 3 shells that broke from the total number of shells Faith had, say, "Since we are going to need to subtract 3 from a larger number, 12, we could use Counting Back to help us if we didn't know what $12 - 3$ was automatically. Let's try it."

Use a number line or a hundred chart to demonstrate and say, "With Counting Back, you use the bigger number as the starting point, then count back. The bigger number is 12, so that is our starting point. Can someone count back 3 for us to get the answer?" Be sure the volunteer says, "11, 10, 9." Emphasize that 12, the starting point, is not counted. End by saying, "Faith has 9 seashells left unbroken."

Next, do some oral Counting Back practice with a variety of numbers. Start with a number line or hundred chart, then move to completing the process mentally. Use examples like "Let's start at 7, what would be 3 less? Let's start at 29, what would be 3 less?"

Finally, list these five subtraction facts on the board: $7 - 3$, $16 - 8$, $48 - 2$, $9 - 5$, and $6 - 0$. Explain, "Counting Back would be efficient with some of these facts but not with others. Which would be good for the Counting Back strategy?" (*7 – 3 and 48 – 2*) Have students verbalize the process as they solve the problems. Point out, "One of the facts has a zero in it ($6 - 0$). That makes it a zero fact, and so there is no need to count back. When using the Zero Strategy the difference always equals the number you are starting with ($6 - 0 = 6$)."

ACTIVITY: Zoo Stamps Sale

Distribute journals, three counters, and a copy of the Zoo Stamps page (p. 72) to each student.

Tell students, "Your next assignment has arrived. The Zoo Zone has decided to have a special sale on zoo stamps. They expect a lot of customers, so they want to be prepared ahead of time by listing the sale prices of the stamps. The workers have sent a sheet that shows the stamps and their original prices. They have also included a description of the sale and how much the customers will save on the prices of certain stamps."

Review the Zoo Stamps page together. To ensure students understand the task, ask, "Who can tell us what the Zoo Zone workers are asking us to do?" (*Figure out the sale price of each of the 10 stamps and make a master list of the prices to use in the gift shop*) "How will we find the sale price of each stamp?" (*By subtracting how many cents off you get from the stamp's original price*) "Why is the Counting Back strategy useful here?" (*Because we are subtracting 1, 2, or 3 from a larger number*)

Model on the board how to show the subtraction for this task. Say, "This is how I'd like you to show your 'math thinking' today. I am going to cut out the lion stamp along with its original price of 9 cents and glue it on separate paper. For this lion stamp, the original price is 9 cents and if I look at the sale details, I see that lion stamps are 1 cent off during the sale. I need to subtract 1 cent from the original price of 9 cents to find the sale price. If I was going to use the Counting Back strategy to do this subtraction, which number would be my starting point?" (*9, because it is the original price*) Draw a number line and demonstrate Counting Back. Finish by writing the equation underneath (or near) the lion stamp:

$$9 - 1 = 8 \text{ cents} \qquad 8 \quad \boxed{9¢}$$

Instruct students to complete the rest of the subtraction in their journals, using the procedure you modeled above. Circulate as they work to make sure everyone is physically completing the Counting Back and showing an understanding of the concept.

To conclude the lesson, gather as a class and use your copy of the Zoo Stamps sheet to make a master list for the Zoo Zone workers. Students should bring their journals in order to check their work and contribute to the discussion. On the master list, simply cross off the original prices and write the sale prices underneath each stamp.

Teaching Tip

Visualize

It is helpful to provide students with some ideas on how to use the Counting Back strategy. You can encourage students to visualize a number line and "hop backward." You can also suggest that they picture the larger number and a set of 1, 2, or 3 dots to count back on. Ask students to talk about what they do or see in their heads when they count back.

Materials

For each pair of students:

- 1 set of Animal Memory Cards, copied on red paper (p. 76)
- 1 set of Egg Memory Cards, copied on blue paper (p. 77)
- 1 copy of the Eggsactly Related Recording Sheet (p. 75)
- pencils
- Practice Page #13 (p. 78)
- Review Page #13 (p. 79)

Literature Links

The Grapes of Math: Mind-Stretching Math Riddles by Greg Tang (Scholastic, 2001)

The riddles in this book challenge children to think creatively by showing them valuable strategies for exploring numbers. Children learn to think strategically, finding convenient sums to make counting easier. The relationship between addition and subtraction is highlighted as a problem solving strategy.

Math for All Seasons: Mind-Stretching Math Riddles by Greg Tang (Scholastic, 2002)

More clever problem solving based on poems and colorful illustrations. The book's riddles encourage kids to think through problems as they transition from counting to arithmetic, introducing ways to group and add numbers. Strategic thinking and related addition and subtraction are interwoven in the mathematical riddles.

ACTIVITY LESSON #13

Eggsactly Related

(SUBTRACTION STRATEGY: USING ADDITION TO SUBTRACT)

Overview: Students use related addition facts to help solve subtraction problems.

Tell the class, "The Zoo Zone needs your help to fix a big problem. Many of the eggs at the zoo have been mixed up and they need to be matched up with their correct animal mothers."

Say, "When you work on this task you will be playing a memory card game." Model the game with a student as you continue to explain. "You will be matching one animal card from the red set to one egg card from the blue set. Select a red animal card first, look at the subtraction fact, and then try to match a blue card with its related addition fact. For example, $6 - 2 = ?$ would match with $2 + 4 = 6$. Once you have found two cards that are related, place them in a match pile. Next it is your partner's turn to place any matches he or she finds in the same pile. Continue alternating turns until all matches are found. At the end of the game work together to record your results on the Eggsactly Related Recording Sheet."

Explain, "Completing this job for the zoo will help you learn how knowing addition facts can help you to solve related subtraction facts."

Pair up students. Pass out the red animal memory cards (p. 76) and the blue egg memory cards (p. 77) to each group. Also give each student a copy of the Eggsactly Related Recording Sheet. Explain that this sheet is where they will record which animal goes with which egg. Tell students to lay out the red cards in columns and rows and the blue cards in columns and rows beside them. All cards should be placed facedown. Remind partners that when they play, they will not record their results until all matches are found and the game is over.

To conclude the lesson, gather as a class to make a master list for the Zoo Zone workers. Students should bring their recording sheets and sit next to their partner in order to check their work and contribute to the discussion. On the master list, make a chart with headings for the mother animal, the amount of eggs, and the related addition and subtraction sentences. Tell students, "The Zoo Zone workers will be 'eggstremely' grateful that you cracked this mystery for them."

Part 3: Two- and Three-Digit Operations

Fishy Addition

(*Introducing the Third Zoo Zone Letter and Two- and Three-Digit Addition Without Regrouping*)

> Overview: Students use place value prompts to add two- and three-digit numbers, without regrouping.

The next group of lessons focuses on two-and three-digit addition and subtraction, both with and without regrouping. Before starting the lessons in Part 3, distribute the third letter from the Zoo Zone to students in the suggested way described in Activity Lesson #1 (p. 8).

Activity: **Two- and Three-Digit Addition Without Regrouping**

Tell students that they are now ready to work on their first task for the Awesome Aquarium. Distribute a copy of the Tank Work Mat (p. 81) and Fish Shipping Form 1 (p. 82) to each pair of students and sets of multilink cubes to work areas.

Say, "The Awesome Aquarium is getting 2 new shipments of fish. They need your help in organizing the fish into tanks. If you look on your Tank Work Mat you will see that the Awesome Aquarium has 3 tanks. The 3 tanks are set up much like the ones, tens, and hundreds places. As you can see, the holding tank can hold up to 9 fish at a time. When we think about place value, what place is this tank like? (*ones place*) The main tank can hold anywhere from 10 to 99 fish, but no more or no less. Which place does this tank represent? (*tens place*) Finally, the giant tank can hold anywhere from 100 to 999 fish, but no more or no less. This is like the hundreds place. The tank rules are very important, and you must follow them when doing your addition to help organize the fish."

Explain to the students that it is their job to add together the two shipments from Fish Shipping Form 1 by using blocks to represent the numbers and prove that the addition is correct.

Materials

For each student:
- Letter #14 (p. 80)
- Practice Page #14 (p. 83)
- Review Page #14 (p. 84)
- pencil

For each pair of students:
- Tank Work Mat (p. 81)
- Fish Shipping Form 1 (p. 82)

For teacher:
- Transparencies of the Tank Work Mat and Fish Shipping Form 1
- class set of multilink cubes
- overhead markers

Teaching Tip

Digi-Blocks: A New Math Manipulative

If available, digi-blocks are a newer math manipulative that is very useful. Not only do they provide a way to represent multiple-digit numbers, but they also force students to recognize the rules of each place in a number. For example, ten digi-blocks must be placed into the tens case in order for it to lock. This shows students that ones cannot be regrouped into a group of ten until exactly ten are available. Because digi-blocks may not be readily available to you, multilink cubes can be substituted. For more information on digi-blocks, go to http://www.digi-block.com.

Teaching Tip

The Value of Manipulatives

When practicing addition and subtraction strategies, some students may inform you that they already know their facts. Acknowledge that they may have their facts memorized, but in order to prove that they completely understand the concept they should also be able to use the manipulatives to prove the accuracy of their thinking. Using manipulatives provides students a way to explore concepts in a concrete way and provide proof and verification that their number work is correct.

Materials

For each student:
- Practice Page #15 (p. 86)
- Review Page #15 (p. 87)
- pencil

For each pair of students:
- Tank Work Mat (p. 81)
- Fish Shipping Form 2 (p. 85)

For teacher:
- Transparencies of the Tank Work Mat and Fish Shipping Form 2
- class set of multilink cubes
- overhead markers

Model how to add the first two shipments (12 + 24) to get the total of 36, using the blocks and an overhead copy of the Tank Work Mat. Show the number 12 by placing 1 tens block in the main tank column and 2 ones in the holding tank column. (If using digi-blocks, be sure to show your students that 10 blocks are packed inside each tens case.) Next, show 24 by placing 2 tens blocks in the main tank and 4 ones in the holding tank directly below the other blocks.

Again, model how to combine the ones place and then the tens place for a total of 36. Switch to the overhead copy of the Fish Shipping Form and show how to record the number sentence 12 + 24 = 36 fish in the space provided. Explain to the students that their job is to complete the rest of the form in the same manner. Point out that some of the numbers are three-digit numbers, meaning that they will need to pay attention to the hundreds column and use the giant tank as well. Circulate as the students work in pairs and be sure to have them demonstrate a problem for you.

ACTIVITY LESSON #15

More Fishy Addition

(Two- and Three-Digit Addition With and Without Regrouping)

Overview: Students use place value prompts to add two- and three-digit numbers, with and without regrouping.

Say, "In your first task for the Awesome Aquarium, you added two shipments of fish to get a total that would help the aquarium workers organize their tanks. Since you were so successful, the aquarium workers are asking for your help again. Additional fish are being shipped to the aquarium. The numbers are getting larger, so fish will need to be regrouped into the main and giant tanks in order to keep the fish healthy and thriving."

Model a solution to the following problem with students:

> There are already 27 angelfish in the main and holding tanks. 17 more are arriving today. How many angelfish will the Awesome Aquarium need to house in the main tank and the holding tank? How many angelfish will they have in all the tanks?"

Use the overhead copy of the Tank Work Mat along with manipulatives to work out this problem with the help of student volunteers. Have one student make the 27 angelfish already in the tanks (7 ones in the holding tank and 2 tens in the main tank). Have a second volunteer make the 17 additional angelfish right below the first set (7 ones in the holding tank and 1 ten in the main tank). Remind students that the ones column (or the fish in the holding tank) needs to be added first. Push the blocks together, making 14. Comment on the problem that the holding tank has too many fish. It only allows up to 9, and there are 14. Ask the students how to solve this problem.

If the students do not suggest "regrouping" 10 ones into a ten and moving it to the tens column, or main tank, demonstrate how to do so. Complete the addition by pushing the 2 tens from the 27, the 1 ten from the 17, and the "regrouped" ten from the ones place together to get a total of 40 and the remaining 4 ones, equaling 44 fish. Record with a vertical number sentence that shows the regrouping.

Explain to the students that they will need to look at a shipping form and add together two shipments, like they did in the previous task. They will need to show their number sentences on the shipment form after working out the addition with the blocks. Tell students that some of the addition may require regrouping while some might not, so they will need to work carefully. You might want to work through the first two shipments listed on the form together with your class. This will give you a chance to model regrouping into the hundreds.

ACTIVITY LESSON #16

Tank Overload

(TWO- AND THREE-DIGIT SUBTRACTION WITHOUT REGROUPING)

Overview: Students use place value prompts to subtract two- and three-digit numbers, without regrouping.

Tell students, "You did such a great job with organizing the tanks for the Awesome Aquarium that the fish are very healthy and thriving. In fact, the tanks are beginning to get a bit crowded! The owners have decided to share their fish with another zoo that also wishes to add an aquarium. The Awesome Aquarium has sent a list of how many fish of each type are currently in the tanks as well as a

Teaching Tip

Why Work In Pairs?

Partners working together on math can be a very advantageous arrangement for everyone. Partnerships foster a supportive, nonthreatening learning situation for each student. It also provides students an opportunity to verbalize and discuss what they are learning, which helps to solidify concepts and skills. Struggling students gain support from peers, while more capable students solidify their knowledge by "teaching" a peer. Always require both partners to record the work and answers on individual sheets, and be prepared to explain all work.

Materials

For each pair of students:
- Tank Work Mat (p. 81)
- Fish Removal Form 1 (p. 88)
- set of 0 – 9 digit cards
- pencils
- Practice Page #16 (p. 89)
- Review Page #16 (p. 90)

For teacher:
- Transparencies of the Tank Work Mat, Fish Removal Form 1, and digit cards
- class set of multilink cubes
- overhead markers

Teaching Tip

Audio Option

Another engaging way of presenting the fish removal data is to record an adult dictating the original numbers of each kind of fish and how many need to be removed. Students listen to the recording and take notes in their math journals instead of utilizing the Fish Removal sheet. Providing a recording of problem data focuses and motivates students. It is a different and fun format to try.

list of how many of those fish need to be removed and shipped. (Show overhead copy of the Fish Removal Form 1) Your job is to determine how many of each type of fish will be left in the tanks at the Awesome Aquarium."

Explain, "To work this out, you will be using blocks to represent the number of fish currently in the tanks. Then you will be removing the fish being sent to the other zoo by taking blocks away from the original amount. If there are not enough blocks in the tank you are working on, you will need to take some, or regroup, from the larger tank beside it in order to complete your subtraction. Let's try a practice example."

Present the following problem:

> There were 27 clown fish swimming in the tanks at the Awesome Aquarium. The tank workers decided to send 13 of them over to the new zoo. How many clown fish were left in the Awesome Aquarium's tanks?

Use your overhead copy of the Tank Work Mat to model the subtraction as you work through this problem with the class. Begin by asking the class how many clown fish are already in the tanks. (27) Place 27 blocks on the work mat by putting down 2 tens in the "main tank" and 7 ones in the "holding tank." Ask a volunteer to state how many fish should be removed. (13) Have another volunteer tell the class how many tens and ones make up the number 13. (1 ten and 3 ones) Use digit cards to represent this second number. It is important that the number being subtracted is represented in some way. Some students may initially try to represent this number with blocks, and this creates a great deal of confusion. Digit cards help make the process clearer.

Explain that, just as in addition, it is usually easier to focus on the ones column first. The first step in this subtraction problem is taking away the 3 ones from the 7 ones that are currently in the holding tank. It's important to ask the students if there are enough blocks to do the subtraction in this column. Students need to develop the habit of checking to see that there are enough ones, tens, or hundreds before they begin subtracting.

In this example, students should conclude that there are enough blocks, because 7 is a larger number than 3. Remove 3 ones from the ones column (or "holding tank") and the "3" digit card. Ask how many remain. *(4)* Simultaneously record the subtraction you are modeling with a number sentence. Next have students focus on the tens column (or "main tank"). Ask how many tens need to be taken away from the original 2 tens. *(1 ten)* Again, remember to ask if there are enough to do the subtraction, which there are. *(2 tens − 1 ten = 1 ten)* Model this by removing a tens block from the "main tank" and the accompanying "1" digit card. Pose the final question, "So how many clown fish will be left in the tanks at the Awesome Aquarium?" *(14 clown fish)* Complete the subtraction sentence, adding the label "clown fish" to your answer.

Work through this next problem as student volunteers manipulate the blocks and record the results with a number sentence:

> At the Awesome Aquarium, 126 blue tang fish darted around the tanks. The workers decided to ship 15 to the other zoo. How many blue tang fish were left darting around the tanks at the Awesome Aquarium?

After you have worked together to solve this problem, distribute a copy of Tank Work Mat (p. 81) and the Fish Removal Form 1 (p. 88) to each pair. Also provide sets of blocks to work areas. Use your overhead copy of the Fish Removal sheet to review the format. Remind students that they will find the original number of fish in the tanks listed first and the amount being removed underneath it. They must use their blocks to work out the problem before they record the amount of fish left in the Awesome Aquarium's tanks.

Literature Link

The M&M's Addition Book
by Barbara Barbieri McGrath,
(Charlesbridge, 2004)

This book uses rhyming text and M&M's as a teaching tool. It begins with an excellent review of counting, sorting , estimating, and basic addition concepts and vocabulary before moving into two-digit addition with and without regrouping. Detailed explanations, labels, and illustrations help to explain and model addition concepts in a fun, kid-friendly manner. Subtraction is introduced near the end as candy is taken away. The final page summarizes all of the concepts covered in the book.

Teaching Tip

Labeling

When working on word problems, students will often supply a solitary number as an answer. Require that all answers to word problems be labeled in order to reinforce the idea that numbers stand for something and have meaning in the context of a problem. This helps students keep track of what the numbers in a problem actually mean and helps develop number sense and accuracy as they work.

Materials

For each pair of students:

- Tank Work Mat (p. 81)
- Fish Removal Form 2 (p. 91)
- set of 0 – 9 digit cards
- pencils
- Practice Page #17 (p. 92)
- Review Page #17 (p. 93)

For teacher:

- Transparencies of the Tank Work Mat, Fish Removal Form 2, and digit cards
- class set of multilink cubes
- overhead markers

ACTIVITY LESSON **#17**

More Fish Removal

(TWO- AND THREE-DIGIT SUBTRACTION WITH AND WITHOUT REGROUPING)

Overview: Students use place value prompts to subtract two- and three-digit numbers, with and without regrouping.

Begin by presenting the following problem to the class:

> There were 32 kissing fish bobbling around the tanks of the Awesome Aquarium. But 16 needed to be shipped to another zoo. How many kissing fish remained at the Awesome Aquarium?

Use your overhead copy of the Tank Work Mat to model the subtraction. Begin by asking, "How many kissing fish are already in the tanks?" (*32*) Place 32 blocks on the work mat by putting down 3 tens in the "main tank" and 2 ones in the "holding tank."

Ask, "How many fish are being removed?" (*16*) Have another student tell the class how many tens and ones make up the number 16. (*1 ten and 6 ones*) Place the digit cards to represent that number.

The first step in this subtraction problem is taking away the 6 ones from the 2 ones that are currently in the holding tank. Ask, "Are there enough ones to do the subtraction in this column?" (*No, there are not enough blocks to complete the subtraction because 2 is less than 6.*)

Pose the question, "What should we do then?" If students do not volunteer it on their own, explain that it will be necessary to regroup by taking a ten block from the "main tank" and moving it over to make use of the 10 ones. Model this for the students and then ask, "Now that we have regrouped, how many ones or blocks are in the ones column or "holding tank?" (*12*) Ask, "Are there enough to do the subtraction now?" (*Yes, 12 − 6 = 6*)

Ask students, "How many tens remain in the tens column or "main tank" now that we have regrouped?" (*2 tens*) Ask, "Are there enough to subtract 1 ten from this column?" (*Yes, 2 tens − 1 ten = 1 ten*) Model this by removing a ten. Simultaneously remove the digit cards and record the subtraction you are modeling with a number sentence.

Pose the final question, "So how many kissing fish will be left in the tanks at the Awesome Aquarium?" (*16 kissing fish*) Again, be sure to complete the subtraction sentence, adding the label "kissing fish" to your answer.

Work through this second example with the class:

> There were 213 butterfly fish blowing bubbles in the tanks at the Awesome Aquarium. The workers sent 25 of these "bubble blowers" over to the new zoo. How many butterfly fish continued to call the Awesome Aquarium their home?

Have volunteers manipulate the blocks and digit cards and record the results with a number sentence.

After you have solved this problem together, distribute a copy of the Tank Work Mat (p. 81), the Fish Removal Form 2 (p. 91), the digit cards, and blocks to each pair. Use your overhead copy of the Fish Removal Form 2 to review the format. Remind students that they will find the original number of fish in the tanks listed first and the amount being removed underneath it. They must use their manipulatives to work out the problem before they record the amount of fish left in the Awesome Aquarium's tanks. Remind students again that they should always ask themselves if they have enough to do the subtraction or if they need to regroup. Be sure to see if students are able to identify when regrouping is necessary and when it is not.

Literature Link

Shark Swimathon
by Stuart J. Murphy
(HarperCollins, 2001)

This picture book features a team of young sharks determined to attend a large swim meet. To do so, they must swim 75 laps by the end of the week. Each day, the coach tallies the number of laps each shark swims, presents a total for the team, and subtracts the total from the previous day's total. The story revolves around how many laps are left after each day of practice. Although data representation and addition are a part of the story, the emphasis is on the two-digit subtraction, with subtraction computations completed by the coach displayed on chart paper throughout the book. This is an entertaining story that is a great supplement to lessons on two-digit subtraction.

Teaching Tip

Encouragement and Reward

At the culmination of the addition and subtraction tasks presented in this book, distribute copies of the Thank-You Letter (p. 94) to students. You also may want to consider a final reward for all the students. In honor of their dedication to relearning and mastering these key skills, it might be nice to throw an animal-themed party. Be sure to include animal crackers!

Name: _____   Date: _____

Dear Students,

    We are writing to enlist your help with opening a new zoo. We want our zoo to run efficiently, while being a place of enjoyment for the animals, zoo workers, and visitors. We would like to invite you to become members of our planning committee.

    This job will take commitment, your best efforts, and lots of math! You will be using addition and subtraction skills to help with planning the variety of animals in the zoo, their habitats, feeding schedules and amounts, and much more. You will be assisting with organizing zoo workers, setting up zoo stores, and creating a happy, safe zoo environment.

    Being a member of the Zoo Zone Planning Committee is an important job, but we know you are up to the challenge. We sincerely hope that you will accept this task and become a part of the Zoo Zone Team!

                                        Sincerely,

                                        Mr. Ty Gur
                                        President
                                        Zoo Zone

Reteaching Math: Addition & Subtraction © 2008 by Bob Krech, Scholastic Teaching Resources

Name: _____   Date: _____

Altered Double Ten Frame

Name: _____ Date: _____

Sums Exploration Chart

Using only single-digit addends, how many ways can you find to make these sums?
First, make them on the Altered Double Ten Frame.
Next, write them on this chart. (The first one has been done for you.)
Then, color them in on your 100 Addition Facts Table as you find them.

Sum	# of ways
0	1
0 + 0	

Sum	# of ways
1	

Sum	# of ways
2	

Sum	# of ways
3	

Sum	# of ways
4	

Sum	# of ways
5	

Sum	# of ways
6	

Sum	# of ways
7	

Sum	# of ways
8	

Sum	# of ways
9	

Reteaching Math: Addition & Subtraction © 2008 by Bob Krech, Scholastic Teaching Resources

Name: _____ Date: _____

Sums Exploration Chart

(continued)

Sum	# of ways
10	

Sum	# of ways
11	

Sum	# of ways
12	

Sum	# of ways
13	

Sum	# of ways
14	

Sum	# of ways
15	

Sum	# of ways
16	

Sum	# of ways
17	

Sum	# of ways
18	

Sum	# of ways
19	

Name: _____ Date: _____

100 Addition Facts Table

+	0	1	2	3	4	5	6	7	8	9
0	0 + 0	0 + 1	0 + 2	0 + 3	0 + 4	0 + 5	0 + 6	0 + 7	0 + 8	0 + 9
1	1 + 0	1 + 1	1 + 2	1 + 3	1 + 4	1 + 5	1 + 6	1 + 7	1 + 8	1 + 9
2	2 + 0	2 + 1	2 + 2	2 + 3	2 + 4	2 + 5	2 + 6	2 + 7	2 + 8	2 + 9
3	3 + 0	3 + 1	3 + 2	3 + 3	3 + 4	3 + 5	3 + 6	3 + 7	3 + 8	3 + 9
4	4 + 0	4 + 1	4 + 2	4 + 3	4 + 4	4 + 5	4 + 6	4 + 7	4 + 8	4 + 9
5	5 + 0	5 + 1	5 + 2	5 + 3	5 + 4	5 + 5	5 + 6	5 + 7	5 + 8	5 + 9
6	6 + 0	6 + 1	6 + 2	6 + 3	6 + 4	6 + 5	6 + 6	6 + 7	6 + 8	6 + 9
7	7 + 0	7 + 1	7 + 2	7 + 3	7 + 4	7 + 5	7 + 6	7 + 7	7 + 8	7 + 9
8	8 + 0	8 + 1	8 + 2	8 + 3	8 + 4	8 + 5	8 + 6	8 + 7	8 + 8	8 + 9
9	9 + 0	9 + 1	9 + 2	9 + 3	9 + 4	9 + 5	9 + 6	9 + 7	9 + 8	9 + 9

Reteaching Math: Addition & Subtraction © 2008 by Bob Krech, Scholastic Teaching Resources

Name: _____   Date: _____

Primate Shipping Form

The following numbers of primates will be shipped to the Zoo Zone. Please remember that each primate will need a playmate. It is important to keep that in mind when planning their habitats.

Primates	Number
gorillas	5
tamarinds	8
baboons	2
mandrills	4
gibbons	1
chimpanzees	7
orangutans	9
New World monkeys	3
orange apes	6

Name: _____   Date: _____

WORD PROBLEM

Jessica was making a monkey cake for her birthday party. The recipe would not be enough to feed all the guests. Jessica needed to double the recipe by doubling each of the ingredients. If the original recipe called for: 1 box of cake mix, 2 cups of chocolate chips, 3 eggs, and 4 tablespoons of oil, how much of each ingredient will Jessica need to use?

BASICS BOX

To help Jessica, you will need to use the Doubles strategy. *Doubles* means the number in each group you are adding is the same. For example: $5 + 5 = 10$. You are adding 5 in one group to 5 in another group. Your total is 10, the double of 5.

●●●●● + ○○○○○ = ●●●●●
○○○○○

Jessica will need:

$1 + 1 = 2$ boxes of cake mix

$2 + 2 = 4$ cups of chocolate chips

$3 + 3 = 6$ eggs

$4 + 4 = 8$ tablespoons of oil

PRACTICE

Add using the Doubles strategy. Write the sum.

1. $7 + 7 =$ _____

2. $6 + 6 =$ _____

3. $4 + 4 =$ _____

4. $9 + 9 =$ _____

5. $8 + 8 =$ _____

6. $3 + 3 =$ _____

Solve the riddle. Use Doubles.

7. We are 2 spiders. How many legs do we have? _____

JOURNAL

How can you use your Doubles fact $6 + 6$ to help you with $60 + 60$ or $600 + 600$? Explain your thinking with pictures, numbers, or words.

Name: _____ Date: _____

Write the sums for these Doubles facts.

1. 7 + 7 = _____

2. 8 + 8 = _____

3. 5 + 5 = _____

4. 9 + 9 = _____

5. 70 + 70 = _____

6. 80 + 80 = _____

7. 50 + 50 = _____

8. 90 + 90 = _____

9.   2
      + 2
     ____

10.   4
       + 4
      ____

11.   3
       + 3
      ____

12.   20
       + 20
      ____

13.   40
       + 40
      ____

14.   30
       + 30
      ____

Double these numbers. Write the answers on the line.

15. 10 _____   **17.** 20 _____   **19.** 5 _____

16. 8 _____   **18.** 1 _____   **20.** 7 _____

The following numbers were doubled. What were the original numbers?
Write them on the lines.

21. 10 _____   **23.** 6 _____   **25.** 12 _____

22. 18 _____   **24.** 2 _____   **26.** 4 _____

Name: _____   Date: _____

Math Secret # _____

_____

PICTURE EXAMPLE

WORDS

_____

_____

_____

_____

_____

EQUATION EXAMPLES

Reteaching Math: Addition & Subtraction © 2008 by Bob Krech, Scholastic Teaching Resources

Playtime Pairing

Materials:

1 game board and 1 set of animal cards per pair of students

1 Toy Order Form recording sheet per student

How to Play:

1. Shuffle animal cards and place them facedown.

2. Player 1 chooses a card and counts the number of animals on it. Player 1 must tell Player 2 the Doubles fact for that number. If Player 2 agrees, Player 1 then pairs the animal card to the related Doubles Plus One fact on the game board. This will reveal which toy should be ordered for that animal's habitat. Player 2 should check to see if the placement is correct.

3. Players continue taking turns until all the spaces on the game board are full.

4. Both players should complete the Toy Order Form for the Zoo Zone Company.

$\begin{array}{r} 6 \\ + 7 \\ \hline \end{array}$ $\begin{array}{r} 7 \\ + 6 \\ \hline \end{array}$ **rope ladders**	$\begin{array}{r} 4 \\ + 5 \\ \hline \end{array}$ $\begin{array}{r} 5 \\ + 4 \\ \hline \end{array}$ **tubes**
$\begin{array}{r} 2 \\ + 3 \\ \hline \end{array}$ $\begin{array}{r} 3 \\ + 2 \\ \hline \end{array}$ **rubber fish**	$\begin{array}{r} 8 \\ + 9 \\ \hline \end{array}$ $\begin{array}{r} 9 \\ + 8 \\ \hline \end{array}$ **swings**
$\begin{array}{r} 5 \\ + 6 \\ \hline \end{array}$ $\begin{array}{r} 6 \\ + 5 \\ \hline \end{array}$ **balls**	$\begin{array}{r} 7 \\ + 8 \\ \hline \end{array}$ $\begin{array}{r} 8 \\ + 7 \\ \hline \end{array}$ **color hoops**
$\begin{array}{r} 3 \\ + 4 \\ \hline \end{array}$ $\begin{array}{r} 4 \\ + 3 \\ \hline \end{array}$ **slides**	$\begin{array}{r} 1 \\ + 2 \\ \hline \end{array}$ $\begin{array}{r} 2 \\ + 1 \\ \hline \end{array}$ **scratching logs**

Reteaching Math: Addition & Subtraction © 2008 by Bob Krech, Scholastic Teaching Resources

lion

penguins

walruses

prairie dogs

sea lions

chimpanzees

snakes

baboons

Name: _____ Date: _____

Toy Order Form

Animal	Toy	Number of Toys
baboons		
chimpanzees		
lions		
penguins		
snakes		
prairie dogs		
sea lions		
walruses		

Name: _____ Date: _____

Danny was feeding his fish. He fed 7 goldfish in one tank and 8 tropical fish in another tank. How many fish did Danny feed in total?

BASICS BOX

To solve this problem, you can use the Doubles Plus One addition strategy because 7 + 8 is one away from a Double. To use the Doubles Plus One strategy, you double the smaller number and add 1. When adding 7 + 8, think of the Doubles fact for 7, the smaller number: 7 + 7 = 14. Then add 1 to get the sum for 7 + 8: 7 + 8 = 15.

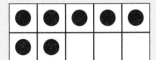 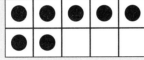

Double   Doubles Plus One

7 + 7 = 14   7 + 8 = 15

If you know that 7 + 7 = 14, then 7 + 8 = 15. Danny must feed 15 fish in total.

PRACTICE

Use the Doubles Plus One strategy to add. Circle the number you would double.
Say the Double to yourself, then write the Doubles Plus One.

1. ⑥ + 7 = __13__

2. 8 + 9 = _____

3. 5 + 4 = _____

4. 3 + 4 = _____

5. 2
   + 3
   ____

6. 6
   + 5
   ____

7. 9
   + 8
   ____

8. 8
   + 7
   ____

JOURNAL

Write an addition story problem that uses a Doubles Plus One fact.
Be sure to include your answer. Look at Danny's fish problem for an example.

Name: _____   Date: _____

Circle the number you would double. Then solve and write the sums for these Doubles Plus One facts.

1. 6 + 7 = _____

2. 7 + 8 = _____

3. 5 + 6 = _____

4. 1 + 2 = _____

5. 7 + 6 = _____

6. 5 + 4 = _____

7. $\begin{array}{r} 8 \\ + 9 \\ \hline \end{array}$

8. $\begin{array}{r} 2 \\ + 3 \\ \hline \end{array}$

9. $\begin{array}{r} 4 \\ + 5 \\ \hline \end{array}$

10. $\begin{array}{r} 3 \\ + 4 \\ \hline \end{array}$

11. $\begin{array}{r} 9 \\ + 8 \\ \hline \end{array}$

12. $\begin{array}{r} 6 \\ + 5 \\ \hline \end{array}$

13. $\begin{array}{r} 4 \\ + 3 \\ \hline \end{array}$

14. $\begin{array}{r} 8 \\ + 7 \\ \hline \end{array}$

Look at each Doubles fact below. Write the 2 Doubles Plus One facts it helps you solve.

15. 5 + 5 _____ and _____   16. 8 + 8 _____ and _____

Mixed Practice: Solve each Double and Double Plus One fact. Write the sums.

17. 6 + 6 = _____

18. 6 + 7 = _____

19. 7 + 6 = _____

20. 60 + 60 = _____

21. 60 + 70 = _____

22. 70 + 60 = _____

23. 4 + 4 = _____

24. 4 + 5 = _____

25. 5 + 4 = _____

26. 40 + 40 = _____

27. 40 + 50 = _____

28. 50 + 40 = _____

Name: _____   Date: _____

Petting Zoo Inventory

The following animals need to be placed in the Children's Petting Zoo section of the Zoo Zone. There can be no more than 10 animals in one pen. Animals that are listed together must remain together. (For example: pigs, 5 means that the 5 pigs must stay together in one pen.) All animals must be placed. Please use the Petting Zoo Pens sheet to show your placement of the animals.

Animals	Number
pigs	5
rabbits	3
sheep	6
llamas	2
ponies	4
cows	1
donkeys	7
goats	9
ducks	8
geese	5

Name: _____   Date: _____

Petting Zoo Pens

Pen 1

Pen 2

Pen 3

Pen 4

Pen 5

Reteaching Math: Addition & Subtraction © 2008 by Bob Krech, Scholastic Teaching Resources

Name: _____   Date: _____

WORD PROBLEM

Lilly was adding new zoo stamps to her collection book. Each page of her book holds 10 stamps. Lilly put 3 lion stamps and 4 tiger stamps on one page. How many more stamps could Lilly put on that page to make exactly 10?

BASICS BOX

To solve this problem you can use the Make Ten strategy, Lilly already put 3 lion stamps and 4 tiger stamps on the page. 3 + 4 makes 7 stamps already on the page. The page can only hold 10. Think of what you know about combinations of 10. 7 and _____ make 10, so Lilly can put 3 more stamps on the page until it is full.

3 + 4 = 7 stamps

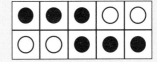

7 + _____ = 10

PRACTICE

Use the Make Ten strategy. Write the other part of 10.

6 +		= 10
8 +		= 10
1 +		= 10
3 +		= 10
5 +		= 10
4 +		= 10
2 +		= 10

JOURNAL

If Lilly had 4 Zebra stamps, 2 elephant stamps, and 5 peacock stamps, could she fit them all on one page? Why or why not? Explain your reasoning with words and show your math with pictures and numbers.

55

Name: _____ Date: _____

List the ways to make ten using single-digit addends in the chart below.

addend	+ addend	= sum of 10

Mixed Practice: Solve. Write the sums.

1. 4 + 6 = _____   **5.** 5 + 5 = _____   **9.** 9 + 9 = _____

2. 8 + 7 = _____   **6.** 4 + 5 = _____   **10.** 4 + 4 = _____

3. 7 + 7 = _____   **7.** 7 + 3 = _____   **11.** 8 + 9 = _____

4. 2 + 8 = _____   **8.** 1 + 9 = _____   **12.** 6 + 5 = _____

13.　　6　　　　**15.**　　7　　　　**17.**　　3　　　　**19.**　　3
　　　　+ 6　　　　　　　　+ 6　　　　　　　　+ 2　　　　　　　　+ 7
　　　　‾‾‾‾　　　　　　　‾‾‾‾　　　　　　　‾‾‾‾　　　　　　　‾‾‾‾

14.　　2　　　　**16.**　　3　　　　**18.**　　9　　　　**20.**　　8
　　　　+ 2　　　　　　　　+ 3　　　　　　　　+ 1　　　　　　　　+ 8
　　　　‾‾‾‾　　　　　　　‾‾‾‾　　　　　　　‾‾‾‾　　　　　　　‾‾‾‾

Reteaching Math: Addition & Subtraction © 2008 by Bob Krech, Scholastic Teaching Resources

Name: _____ Date: _____

Special Additions Work Mat

Place
game card
here.

Name: _____   Date: _____

toucans

9 adults + 1 baby

roadrunners

9 adults + 2 babies

hummingbirds

9 adults + 3 babies

cockatoos

9 adults + 4 babies

ostriches

9 adults + 5 babies

macaws

9 adults + 6 babies

emus

9 adults + 7 babies

bald eagles

9 adults + 8 babies

penguins

9 adults + 9 babies

Reteaching Math: Addition & Subtraction © 2008 by Bob Krech, Scholastic Teaching Resources

Name: _____ Date: _____

Special Additions Recording Sheet

Please use the Special Additions Game Cards and work mat to figure out how many of each bird species the Zoo Zone Bird Sanctuary workers need to order supplies for. The cards will tell you how many babies will be joining the 9 adults at the zoo. Draw cards at random, and use the work mat to do your math. Please record your totals below.

Bird Species	Species Total (Adults + Babies = Total)
toucans	_____ + _____ = _____
roadrunners	_____ + _____ = _____
hummingbirds	_____ + _____ = _____
cockatoos	_____ + _____ = _____
ostriches	_____ + _____ = _____
macaws	_____ + _____ = _____
emus	_____ + _____ = _____
bald eagles	_____ + _____ = _____
penguins	_____ + _____ = _____

Name: _____ Date: _____

WORD PROBLEM

Aji went to the candy store with his mom. He had 9 cents in his pocket. He needed to ask his mom for 6 more cents to buy a bubble gum lollipop. How much did the bubble gun lollipop cost?

BASICS BOX

To find out how much the lollipop costs, you need to add the 9 cents Aji had in his pocket to the 6 cents his mom gave him. Together, Aji then had enough to buy the lollipop he wanted. $9 + 6$ is a nines fact, so you can use the Special Nines strategy to do the addition.

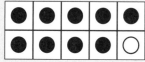

Use one of the 6 you are adding to fill the Ten Frame and make ten. There are five more left outside of the Ten Frame. $9 + 6$ is like 10 and 5 more. It equals 15.

Aji's bubble gum lollipop costs 15 cents.

PRACTICE

Add using the Special Nines strategy. Write the sum.

1. $9 + 1 =$ _____

2. $6 + 9 =$ _____

3. $9 + 4 =$ _____

4. $9 + 7 =$ _____

5.
$$\begin{array}{r} 9 \\ +\ 5 \\ \hline \end{array}$$

6.
$$\begin{array}{r} 8 \\ +\ 9 \\ \hline \end{array}$$

7.
$$\begin{array}{r} 9 \\ +\ 3 \\ \hline \end{array}$$

8.
$$\begin{array}{r} 9 \\ +\ 2 \\ \hline \end{array}$$

JOURNAL

$9 + 9$ is a Doubles fact and a nines fact. Show how you would solve it using the Special Nines strategy with a picture, a number sentence, and words.

Name: _____ Date: _____

Use the Special Nines strategy to solve these problems.

1. $9 + 2 =$ _____

2. $9 + 3 =$ _____

3. $9 + 7 =$ _____

4. $9 + 9 =$ _____

5.
$$\begin{array}{r} 9 \\ + 4 \\ \hline \end{array}$$

6.
$$\begin{array}{r} 5 \\ + 9 \\ \hline \end{array}$$

7.
$$\begin{array}{r} 8 \\ + 9 \\ \hline \end{array}$$

8.
$$\begin{array}{r} 9 \\ + 6 \\ \hline \end{array}$$

Mixed Practice: Solve.

9. $6 + 6 =$ _____

10. $7 + 6 =$ _____

11. $9 + 8 =$ _____

12. $8 + 9 =$ _____

13. $4 + 4 =$ _____

14. $5 + 4 =$ _____

15. $6 + 4 =$ _____

16. $9 + 3 =$ _____

17.
$$\begin{array}{r} 3 \\ + 7 \\ \hline \end{array}$$

18.
$$\begin{array}{r} 8 \\ + 8 \\ \hline \end{array}$$

19.
$$\begin{array}{r} 7 \\ + 8 \\ \hline \end{array}$$

20.
$$\begin{array}{r} 9 \\ + 5 \\ \hline \end{array}$$

21.
$$\begin{array}{r} 7 \\ + 7 \\ \hline \end{array}$$

22.
$$\begin{array}{r} 3 \\ + 4 \\ \hline \end{array}$$

23.
$$\begin{array}{r} 4 \\ + 9 \\ \hline \end{array}$$

24.
$$\begin{array}{r} 7 \\ + 9 \\ \hline \end{array}$$

Name: _____   Date: _____

Harmonious Habitats Recording Sheet

Use your number cards to determine how many animals will be in each habitat listed below. Then, show the two possible combinations for the animals listed in each habitat. You may use each number card only once. Be sure to place cards you have already used in a discard pile. One number card will not be used.

Example:
If you choose number cards 5 and 2 for the arctic, there will be 7 animals in total in the arctic habitat. In the arctic there are polar bears and walruses. So, the two combinations would be

5 polar bears + 2 walruses = 7 animals

2 polar bears + 5 walruses = 7 animals

Habitat	Animal	Number Cards	Equation Combinations ___ + ___ = ___
arctic	polar bears & walruses		
desert	snakes & camels		
rainforest	macaws & eagles		
Australian outback	kangaroos & koala bears		
grasslands	zebras & giraffes		

Reteaching Math: Addition & Subtraction © 2008 by Bob Krech, Scholastic Teaching Resources

Name: _____ Date: _____

Reteaching Math: Addition & Subtraction © 2008 by Bob Krech, Scholastic Teaching Resources

WORD PROBLEM

In the first arctic habitat there are 8 polar bears and 4 walruses. In the second, there are 4 polar bears and 8 walruses. What habitat has more animals? Explain.

BASICS BOX

To solve this problem you can use the Turnaround Partners strategy: $8 + 4 = 12$ animals in total, and $4 + 8 = 12$ animals in total, as well. Joining 2 smaller groups together in any order will result in the same total.

$8 + 4 = 12$ animals

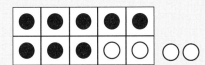

$4 + 8 = 12$ animals

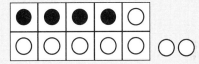

Neither $8 + 4$ nor $4 + 8$ is more. They are both equal. The sum for both equations is 12.

PRACTICE

Write the "turnaround partner" for each problem below and solve.

1. $5 + 4 = $ _____

2. $7 + 6 = $ _____

3. $3 + 7 = $ _____

4. $9 + 2 = $ _____

5. $5 + 3 = $ _____

6. $6 + 8 = $ _____

JOURNAL

Explain what is the same and different about the equations below.

$$2 + 8 = 10 \text{ and } 8 + 2 = 10$$

Name: _____ Date: _____

Write the "turnaround partner" for each equation below and solve.

Equation	Turnaround Partner
5 + 4 = _____	
7 + 8 = _____	
3 + 2 = _____	
9 + 7 = _____	
8 + 9 = _____	
6 + 7 = _____	
9 + 6 = _____	
4 + 9 = _____	

Mixed Practice: Solve.

1. $9 + 9 =$ _____

2. $7 + 6 =$ _____

3. $4 + 6 =$ _____

4. $6 + 6 =$ _____

5. $50 + 50 =$ _____

6. $40 + 60 =$ _____

7. $3 + 4 =$ _____

8. $9 + 5 =$ _____

9. $7 + 3 =$ _____

10. $30 + 30 =$ _____

11. $2 + 9 =$ _____

12. $40 + 40 =$ _____

13.
$$\begin{array}{r} 20 \\ + 20 \\ \hline \end{array}$$

14.
$$\begin{array}{r} 2 \\ + 2 \\ \hline \end{array}$$

15.
$$\begin{array}{r} 7 \\ + 6 \\ \hline \end{array}$$

16.
$$\begin{array}{r} 6 \\ + 3 \\ \hline \end{array}$$

Reteaching Math: Addition & Subtraction © 2008 by Bob Krech, Scholastic Teaching Resources

Name: _____ Date: _____

Shopping List

Please total the amount of each food the Zoo Zone Kitchen workers will need to order by combining how much the main kitchen needs with how much the second kitchen needs.

Food	Main Kitchen	Second Kitchen	Total
carrots	8 pounds	2 pounds	
lettuce	4 heads	2 heads	
kale	9 heads	3 heads	
spinach	5 pounds	3 pounds	
corn	7 ears	3 ears	
mangoes	5 whole mangoes	2 whole mangoes	
melons	6 whole melons	2 whole melons	
meat	6 pounds	3 pounds	
eggs	9 dozen	2 dozen	
apples	8 cases	3 cases	

Name: _____ Date: _____

Alex earned his weekly allowance by doing his chores. He earned $7 for doing the dishes and $2 for taking out the trash. How much money did Alex earn in total for the week?

BASICS BOX

To get the total amount of money that Alex earned for the week, you need to add the $7 he earned for doing the dishes to the $2 he earned for taking out the trash. When adding $7 + $2, you can use the Counting On strategy because it works well when you are adding 1, 2, or 3 to a larger number. You take the bigger number, 7, and "count on" 2 more . . . 8, 9.

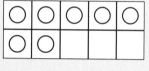

7   +   8, 9

$7 + $2 = $9
Alex earned $9 for his allowance in total.

PRACTICE

Add using the Counting On strategy. Write the sum.

1. 7 + 1 = _____

2. 6 + 2 = _____

3. 4 + 2 = _____

4.   9
    + 3
    ____

5.   8
    + 3
    ____

6. 5 + 3 = _____

7. 46 + 3 = _____

8. 29 + 2 = _____

JOURNAL

Write a story problem to go with this number sentence: 16 + 2 = 18.
Then show how you would solve it using Counting On.

Name: _____   Date: _____

Solve these problems by counting on. Remember to use the bigger number as the starting point!

1. 7 + 2 = _____

5. 7 + 1 = _____

9. 19 + 3 = _____

2. 9 + 3 = _____

6. 6 + 2 = _____

10. 26 + 2 = _____

3. 5 + 1 = _____

7. 11 + 2 = _____

11. 44 + 3 = _____

4. 8 + 3 = _____

8. 17 + 3 = _____

12. 18 + 2 = _____

Mixed Practice: Solve. Circle the equations where counting on was helpful.

13. 26 + 2 = _____

17. 8 + 9 = _____

21. 5 + 2 = _____

14. 7 + 6 = _____

18. 70 + 3 = _____

22. 4 + 4 = _____

15. 9 + 9 = _____

19. 6 + 6 = _____

23. 25 + 1 = _____

16. 8 + 2 = _____

20. 5 + 4 = _____

24. 5 + 3 = _____

25.   6
    + 4
    ____

26.   6
    + 5
    ____

27.   7
    + 7
    ____

28. 36
    + 2
    ____

Name: _____   Date: _____

Animal Addends

Solve the problems below. Be sure to list each addition strategy you use.

Animal Checkups	Strategy Used
6 elephants + 2 rhinos + 4 hippos =	Strategy _____
5 penguins + 2 parrots + 5 gorillas =	Strategy _____
1 swan + 7 camels + 0 snakes + 8 lions =	Strategy _____
9 bears + 4 tigers + 2 turtles =	Strategy _____

Name: _____   Date: _____

Lucia was playing in her backyard and with her friend, Whitney. They decided to go on an insect hunt. After a half an hour, the girls found 7 ladybugs, 5 butterflies, 3 grasshoppers, and 5 meal worms. How many insects did Lucia and Whitney find altogether?

BASICS BOX

To get the total number of insects that the girls found, you need to add "multiple addends." It is best to look at the entire problem and search for easy combinations to add first.

When looking at 7 + 5 + 3 + 5, there are 2 combinations that stand out.

7 + 3 is a way to Make Ten.

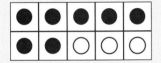

5 + 5 is a Double and a way to Make Ten.

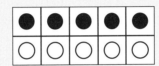

So, if 7 + 3 = 10 and 5 + 5 = 10, just add 10 + 10 to get a total of 20 insects.

PRACTICE

Solve these multiple-addend problems. Look for easy combinations to add first.

1. 5 + 4 + 1 = _____

2. 6 + 6 + 12 = _____

3. 8 + 6 + 4 = _____

4.
```
   3
   3
   3
 + 1
____
```

5.
```
   4
   5
   6
 + 3
____
```

6.
```
   6
   8
   2
 + 6
____
```

JOURNAL

Pretend you are teaching a younger student about solving the problem below. Write a good explanation of your strategies for adding.

8 + 6 + 3 + 7 + 2 =

Name: _____   Date: _____

Use addition strategies like Make Ten to help solve these problems.

1. $3 + 7 + 2 =$ _____   **5.** $7 + 3 + 2 =$ _____   **9.** $9 + 7 + 3 =$ _____

2. $9 + 5 + 1 =$ _____   **6.** $5 + 1 + 4 =$ _____   **10.** $16 + 4 + 2 =$ _____

3. $6 + 1 + 1 =$ _____   **7.** $10 + 2 + 18 =$ _____   **11.** $22 + 22 + 3 =$ _____

4. $6 + 3 + 6 =$ _____   **8.** $17 + 3 + 5 =$ _____   **12.** $18 + 8 + 2 =$ _____

Mixed Practice: Solve.

13. $6 + 5 =$ _____   **16.** $8 + 8 =$ _____   **19.** $35 + 2 =$ _____

14. $3 + 6 =$ _____   **17.** $28 + 3 =$ _____   **20.** $5 + 5 + 7 =$ _____

15. $2 + 9 =$ _____   **18.** $4 + 6 + 6 =$ _____   **21.** $85 + 2 =$ _____

---

22. $\begin{array}{r} 26 \\ + 4 \\ \hline \end{array}$ **23.** $\begin{array}{r} 4 \\ + 5 \\ \hline \end{array}$ **24.** $\begin{array}{r} 6 \\ + 7 \\ \hline \end{array}$ **25.** $\begin{array}{r} 56 \\ + 2 \\ \hline \end{array}$

Name: _____   Date: _____

Dear Students,

When visitors come to the Zoo Zone they always enjoy a stop at our gift shops. We find that we use a great deal of addition and subtraction as we work to supply the shop, keep things organized, and help our shoppers with their purchases. We sell many different items, and lots of them. We find that using subtraction is pretty important, both in the shops and in many other parts of the Zoo Zone.

You've all been such a big help so far, we hope you will continue to lend us your assistance, particularly as we use subtraction. Thank you for your help, and we look forward to continuing our work with you in the Zoo Zone.

Sincerely,

Mr. Ty Gur

President
Zoo Zone

Name: _____   Date: _____

Zoo Stamps

Figure out the sale price of each of the 10 stamps below. The original prices of the zoo stamps are listed under each stamp. Details about the sale prices are in the top box, at right.

Special Sale on Zoo Stamps
monkey stamps = 3 cents off
elephant stamps = 2 cents off
lion stamps = 1 cent off

1.

9 cents

2.

8 cents

3.

7 cents

4.

15 cents

5.

18 cents

6.

16 cents

7.

12 cents

8.

20 cents

9.

25 cents

10.

37 cents

Name: _____ Date: _____

Daniel built a tower that was 16 cubes tall. Kaya built a tower that was 3 cubes shorter than Daniel's. How tall was Kaya's tower?

BASICS BOX

To find out how tall Kaya's tower is, you need to subtract 3 cubes from Daniel's 16 cubes because Kaya's tower is 3 cubes shorter or less than Daniel's. When subtracting $16 - 3$, you can use the Counting Back strategy because it works well when you are subtracting 1, 2, or 3 from a larger number. You would take the bigger number, 16, use it as a starting point, and "count back" 3 . . . 5, 14, 13.

Daniel's cubes ☐☐☐☐☐☐☐☐☐☐☐☐☐☒☒☒ 16 cubes

Kaya's cubes ☐☐☐☐☐☐☐☐☐☐☐☐☐ 13 14 15

$16 - 3 = 13$
Kaya's tower is 13 cubes tall.

PRACTICE

Subtract using the Counting Back strategy. Write the difference.

1. $7 - 1 =$ _____

2. $6 - 2 =$ _____

3. $8 - 2 =$ _____

4.
$$\begin{array}{r} 9 \\ -3 \\ \hline \end{array}$$

5.
$$\begin{array}{r} 7 \\ -3 \\ \hline \end{array}$$

6. $5 - 2 =$ _____

7. $29 - 3 =$ _____

8. $70 - 2 =$ _____

JOURNAL

Would the Counting Back strategy be helpful in solving $73 - 2$ or $65 - 7$? Explain which fact it would be helpful with and why. Explain why it would not be helpful with the other fact.

Name: _____   Date: _____

Solve these problems by counting back. Remember to use the bigger number as the starting point!

1. $8 - 2 =$ _____

2. $7 - 3 =$ _____

3. $5 - 1 =$ _____

4. $8 - 3 =$ _____

5. $9 - 1 =$ _____

6. $6 - 1 =$ _____

7. $12 - 2 =$ _____

8. $17 - 3 =$ _____

9. $19 - 3 =$ _____

10. $46 - 2 =$ _____

11. $74 - 3 =$ _____

12. $18 - 2 =$ _____

Mixed Practice: Solve. Circle the equations where counting back was helpful.

13. $10 - 2 =$ _____

14. $16 - 8 =$ _____

15. $18 - 9 =$ _____

16. $14 - 7 =$ _____

17. $70 - 3 =$ _____

18. $12 - 6 =$ _____

19. $20 - 10 =$ _____

20. $8 - 4 =$ _____

21. $85 - 1 =$ _____

22. $\begin{array}{r} 10 \\ -\ 4 \\ \hline \end{array}$

23. $\begin{array}{r} 36 \\ -\ 3 \\ \hline \end{array}$

24. $\begin{array}{r} 10 \\ -\ 7 \\ \hline \end{array}$

25. $\begin{array}{r} 36 \\ -\ 2 \\ \hline \end{array}$

Reteaching Math: Addition & Subtraction © 2008 by Bob Krech, Scholastic Teaching Resources

Name: _____   Date: _____

Eggsactly Related Recording Sheet

Animal	Egg

Animal Memory Cards

6 − 2 = ?

12 − 5 = ?

9 − 6 = ?

7 − 6 = ?

18 − 9 = ?

10 − 8 = ?

8 − 3 = ?

8 − 2 = ?

9 − 1 = ?

14 − 8 = ?

13 − 6 = ?

11 − 7 = ?

Egg Memory Cards

2 + 4 = 6

4

7 + 5 = 12

7

6 + 3 = 9

3

6 + 1 = 7

1

9 + 9 = 18

9

2 + 8 = 10

2

5 + 3 = 8

5

2 + 6 = 8

6

1 + 8 = 9

8

8 + 6 = 14

6

6 + 7 = 13

7

7 + 4 = 11

4

Name: _____   Date: _____

WORD PROBLEM

Kerri was making a bracelet for her niece, Mary. She had 15 beads on the string, but when she measured it around Mary's wrist, it was too big. Kerri realized that she needed to remove 7 beads to make the bracelet fit Mary's wrist. How many beads were left on Mary's bracelet?

BASICS BOX

Kerri needed to subtract 7 beads from the original 15 beads that she had on the bracelet so that it would fit her niece, Mary. To solve 15 − 7, you could use the related addition fact to get the answer.

Think: 7 + ? = 15 (What is the other part needed to make 15 if you have 7?)

○○○○○○○   ●●●●●●●●

   7   +   8   = 15

The other part is 8, so . . . 15 − 7 = 8

⊖⊖⊖⊖⊖⊖⊖●●●●●●●●

Mary's bracelet had 8 beads left.

PRACTICE

Write a related fact for each addition or subtraction fact below, then solve.

6 + 8 =	
7 + 5 =	
3 + 9 =	
4 + 7 =	
13 − 6 =	
18 − 9 =	
12 − 8 =	
16 − 6 =	

JOURNAL

Write two story problems to go with these related facts: 9 + 8 = 17 and 17 − 9 = 8

Reteaching Math: Addition & Subtraction © 2008 by Bob Krech, Scholastic Teaching Resources

Name: _____   Date: _____

Use the addition facts to write the two related subtraction facts. Then solve.

addition facts	subtraction fact 1	subtraction fact 2
7 + 6 and 6 + 7	13 – 7 = 6	13 – 6 = 7
3 + 7 and 7 + 3		
8 + 3 and 3 + 8		
9 + 7 and 7 + 9		
4 + 5 and 5 + 4		
6 + 9 and 9 + 6		
5 + 2 and 2 + 5		
6 + 8 and 8 + 6		

Mixed Practice: Solve. Write the sums and differences.

1. 8 + 6 = _____

2. 14 – 8 = _____

3. 6 + 8 = _____

4. 2 + 8 = _____

5. 10 – 8 = _____

6. 4 + 3 = _____

7. 7 – 4 = _____

8. 17 – 8 = _____

9. 17 – 9 = _____

10.
```
  16
–  9
____
```

11.
```
   9
+  7
____
```

12.
```
   7
+  9
____
```

13.
```
  16
–  7
____
```

14.
```
  13
–  5
____
```

15.
```
   5
+  8
____
```

16.
```
  13
–  8
____
```

17.
```
   8
+  5
____
```

Name: _____ Date: _____

Dear Students,

   We are writing to thank you for your hard work and dedication to the Zoo Zone. We are quite pleased with how well you have completed all of your assigned tasks. You have made the opening of our new zoo run efficiently. Not only did you handle your assignments in a responsible manner, but you also provided our zoo staff with great math strategies and advice for their future computations and problem-solving tasks.

   Since you have been so helpful up to this point, we'd like to ask for your assistance once again with the newest component of our zoo, the Awesome Aquarium. We have decided to add an aquarium section to our zoo, and organizing the tanks is proving to be difficult. There are certain tank rules we need to follow in order to keep the fish safe and healthy. Setting up the tanks, while obeying the tank rules, means using lots of math, particularly more complicated two- and three-digit addition and subtraction. Since you have proven to be skilled mathematicians, we could really use your help!

   We hope that you will accept this challenge, and we look forward to working with you again!

                              Sincerely,

                              Mr. Ty Gur

                              President
                              Zoo Zone

Reteaching Math: Addition & Subtraction © 2008 by Bob Krech, Scholastic Teaching Resources

Name: _____ Date: _____

Tank Work Mat

Giant Tank 100–999 (hundreds)	Main Tank 10–99 (tens)	Holding Tank 0–9 (ones)

Name: _____   Date: _____

Fish Shipping Form 1

(Awesome Aquarium: Fishy Addition)

Shipment #1	Shipment #2	Total
12	24	
132	46	
37	52	
15	73	
251	123	
303	33	
66	13	
121	68	
54	125	
26	43	

Name: _____ Date: _____

Jack ate the 15 blue M & M's from his bag. Since Jack gave his friend, Jill, the rest of his bag, she gave him the 23 blue M & M's from her bag to eat. How many blue M & M's did Jack have altogether?

BASICS BOX

To find out how many blue M & M's Jack ate altogether, you need to add the 15 he kept from his bag to the 23 he got from Jill. Both of your addends are two-digit numbers, so you need to first add the ones and then the tens.

15 + 23 = 38 M & M's
Jack had 38 blue M & M's.

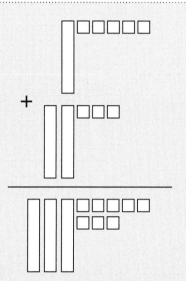

PRACTICE

Add.

1. 45
   + 24
   _____

2. 62
   + 36
   _____

3. 133
   + 56
   _____

4. 275
   + 112
   _____

5. 41 + 28 = _____

6. 13 + 83 = _____

7. 463 + 26 = _____

JOURNAL

If 34 fish were swimming in the tanks at the Awesome Aquarium and 53 more fish were added, how many fish would be in the "holding tank" (or ones column) and how many fish would be in the "main tank" (or tens column)? Show your answer with numbers and by drawing the tanks and fish.

Name: _____ Date: _____

Solve these problems by using addition.
Remember your strategies for more efficient adding. Write the sums.

1.   44 + 44 = _____

2.   32 + 56 = _____

3.   51 + 18 = _____

4.   43 + 53 = _____

5.   22 + 22 = _____

6.   30 + 50 = _____

7.   11 + 58 = _____

8.   14 + 73 = _____

9.   16 + 52 = _____

10. 34 + 23 = _____

11. $\begin{array}{r} 10 \\ + \ 62 \\ \hline \end{array}$

12. $\begin{array}{r} 70 \\ + \ 20 \\ \hline \end{array}$

13. $\begin{array}{r} 100 \\ + \ 99 \\ \hline \end{array}$

14. $\begin{array}{r} 123 \\ + \ 34 \\ \hline \end{array}$

15. $\begin{array}{r} 678 \\ + \ 321 \\ \hline \end{array}$

16. $\begin{array}{r} 125 \\ + \ 824 \\ \hline \end{array}$

Name: _____ Date: _____

Fish Shipping Form 2

(Awesome Aquarium: More Fishy Addition)

Shipment #1	Shipment #2	Total
16	34	
135	65	
17	33	
15	54	
120	183	
208	33	
37	9	
121	19	
54	117	
26	84	

Name: _____ Date: _____

WORD PROBLEM

Lizzie and her sister Olivia were putting together a puzzle at the kitchen table. They had 127 pieces left to place. "I give up! This is too hard!" cried Olivia. "Don't quit. We already put 58 of the pieces together," encouraged Lizzie. Olivia agreed to keep working on the puzzle project. How many pieces did the puzzle have in all?

BASICS BOX

To determine how many pieces the puzzle has in all, you need to add the 127 remaining pieces to the 58 pieces that Lizzie and Olivia already put together.

1. Add the ones.
   (7 + 8 = 15)
2. Regroup 10 of the ones into a ten, leaving 5 ones.
3. Add the tens.
   (1 ten + 2 tens + 5 tens = 8 tens)
4. Add the hundreds.
   (1 hundred + 0 hundreds = 1 hundred)

Lizzie and Olivia's puzzle had 185 pieces.

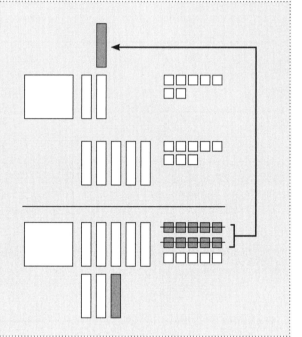

PRACTICE

Add.

1. 48 + 24	**2.** 162 + 46	**3.** 66 + 17	**4.** 375 + 18

5. 47 + 38 = _____   **6.** 18 + 53 = _____   **7.** 107 + 99 = _____

JOURNAL

How do you know when you need to regroup in addition? Explain using pictures, numbers, and words.

Reteaching Math: Addition & Subtraction © 2008 by Bob Krech, Scholastic Teaching Resources

Name: _____   Date: _____

Solve these problems by using addition.
Remember to decide if you need to regroup or not. Write the sums.

1.   79
     + 19
     ———

2.   62
     + 64
     ———

3.   30
     + 53
     ———

4.   90
     + 30
     ———

5. 92 + 28 = _____

6. 73 + 73 = _____

7. 92 + 37 = _____

8. 80 + 60 = _____

9. 10 + 28 = _____

10. 14 + 96 = _____

11. 43 + 57 = _____

12. 31 + 63 = _____

13.   578
     + 18
     ———

14.   627
     + 24
     ———

15.   481
     + 221
     ———

16.   848
     + 161
     ———

Name: _____ Date: _____

Fish Removal Form 1
(Tank Overload)

Fish	Blue Tang	Kissing Fish	Butterfly Fish	Sea Bass	Flounder
Number in Tanks	65	127	87	143	77
Number Removed	34	16	63	21	25
Amount Left in Tanks					

Reteaching Math: Addition & Subtraction © 2008 by Bob Krech, Scholastic Teaching Resources

Name: _____ Date: _____

"Boys, the cookies are ready!" called John and Pete's mom. The twins raced downstairs to enjoy their mom's delicious mini chocolate chip cookies. They ate until they were stuffed! In the end, John ate 28 cookies and Pete ate 16. How many more cookies did John eat than Pete?

BASICS BOX

In this problem you are comparing the number of cookies John ate to the number of cookies that Pete ate. You need to use subtraction to find the difference between the two numbers in order to determine how many more cookies John ate, or even how many fewer cookies Pete ate.

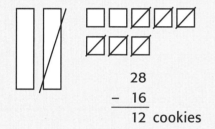

```
   28
 - 16
 ──────
   12  cookies
```

1. Start with the larger number (John's 28 cookies).
2. Subtract the number of cookies Pete ate (16). This is two-digit subtraction, so you must first subtract the ones (8 – 6). Ask yourself, "Are there enough to do the subtraction?" In this case there are, so you can subtract (8 – 6 = 2).
3. Next, subtract the tens. Ask yourself again, "Are there enough, to do the subtraction?" There are, so you can subtract (2 tens – 1 ten = 1 ten).
4. Look at what is left: John ate 12 more cookies than Pete. (Pete also ate 12 fewer cookies than John!)

PRACTICE

Subtract.

1. 85
  – 22
  ─────

2. 67
  – 34
  ─────

3. 185
  – 63
  ─────

4. 294
  – 172
  ─────

5. 29 – 12 = _____

6. 47 – 31 = _____

7. 98 – 57 = _____

JOURNAL

If John and Pete's mom made more cookies and John ate 34 cookies while Pete ate 21, what would be the difference between the number of cookies the boys ate? Show how to solve this problem at least 2 different ways.

Name: _____   Date: _____

Solve these problems by using subtraction.
Remember your strategies for more efficient subtracting. Write the differences.

1.
$$\begin{array}{r} 44 \\ -\,22 \\ \hline \end{array}$$

2.
$$\begin{array}{r} 52 \\ -\,21 \\ \hline \end{array}$$

3.
$$\begin{array}{r} 82 \\ -\,52 \\ \hline \end{array}$$

4.
$$\begin{array}{r} 80 \\ -\,20 \\ \hline \end{array}$$

5. $32 - 11 =$ _____

6. $63 - 43 =$ _____

7. $45 - 33 =$ _____

8. $18 - 13 =$ _____

9. $90 - 60 =$ _____

10. $70 - 30 =$ _____

11. $76 - 55 =$ _____

12. $64 - 43 =$ _____

13.
$$\begin{array}{r} 778 \\ -\,56 \\ \hline \end{array}$$

14.
$$\begin{array}{r} 168 \\ -\,34 \\ \hline \end{array}$$

15.
$$\begin{array}{r} 598 \\ -\,243 \\ \hline \end{array}$$

16.
$$\begin{array}{r} 364 \\ -\,251 \\ \hline \end{array}$$

Name: _____ Date: _____

Fish Removal Form 2

(More Fish Removal)

Fish	Clown Fish	Emperor Angelfish	Barracuda	Angler Fish	Tuna
Number in Tanks	123	63	241	21	311
Number Removed	17	29	63	14	25
Amount Left in Tanks					

Name: _____   Date: _____

Denise went to the gym for a workout. She needed to complete her workout in 45 minutes because she had to meet her friends for dinner and a movie. Denise spent 28 minutes kickboxing before heading over to the weight machines. How much time did she have left to lift weights?

BASICS BOX

In order to figure out how much time Denise has to lift weights, you need to subtract the amount of time she spent kickboxing from the total amount of time she had to work out.

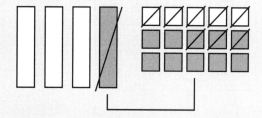

45 − 28 = 17 minutes

1. Start with the total number of minutes Denise had to work out (45 minutes).
2. Subtract the amount of time Denise spent kickboxing (28 minutes). First you must subtract the ones (5 − 8). Ask yourself, "Are there enough to do the subtraction?" In this case there are NOT, so . . .
3. Regroup one of the tens into 10 ones.
4. Now you have enough ones, so you can subtract (15 − 8 = 7).
5. Subtract the tens. Ask yourself, "Are there enough to do the subtraction?" There are, so you can subtract (3 tens − 2 tens = 1 ten).
6. Look at what is left (17).
   Denise has 17 minutes to lift weights.

PRACTICE

Subtract.

1.	82	2.	46	3.	185	4.	264
	− 67		− 15		− 58		− 169

6. 54 − 16 = _____   7. 62 − 41 = _____   8. 92 − 56 = _____

JOURNAL

How do you know when you need to regroup in subtraction?
Explain using pictures, numbers, and words.

Reteaching Math: Addition & Subtraction © 2008 by Bob Krech Scholastic Teaching Resources

Name: _____   Date: _____

Solve these problems by using subtraction.
Remember to decide if you need to regroup or not. Write the differences.

1.   84
        − 42
        ——

2.   72
        − 49
        ——

3.   87
        − 58
        ——

4.   80
        − 34
        ——

5.   67 − 18 = _____

6.   83 − 42 = _____

7.   75
        − 25
        ——

8.   63
        − 14
        ——

9.   80
        − 10
        ——

10.   50
        − 24
        ——

11. 66 − 35 = _____

12. 82 − 34 = _____

13.   468
        − 29
        ——

14.   698
        − 535
        ——

15.   908
        − 36
        ——

16.   564
        − 157
        ——

Name: _____ Date: _____

Dear Students,

We are writing to thank you for all the help you have given us during the opening of the Zoo Zone and the Awesome Aquarium. Our zoo is now running efficiently, and all our animals, zoo workers, and visitors are happy. We would like to thank you for becoming members of our planning committee.

We greatly appreciate your commitment, effort, and math skills! As a result of your hard work, our animals, their habitats, and the zoo shops are thriving.

We are very pleased that you successfully met these challenges with such splendid success! Thank you again for your help and dedication.

Sincerely,

Mr. Ty Gur

President
Zoo Zone

Reteaching Math: Addition & Subtraction © 2008 by Bob Krech, Scholastic Teaching Resources

Activity: Primate Shipping Form (p. 43)

gorillas: 10; tamarinds: 16; baboons: 4; mandrills: 8; gibbon: 2; chimpanzees: 14; orangutans: 18; New World monkeys: 6; orange apes: 12

Practice Page #3 (p. 44)

1. 14
2. 12
3. 8
4. 18
5. 16
6. 6
7. 16

Journal: If you know the answer to the double 6 + 6 = 12 Then you can simply add one zero to the end of 12 to show 3 places, hundredths, for 60 + 60 = 120. For thousandths, add two zeros, for 600 + 600 = 1200.

Review Page #3 (p. 45)

1. 14
2. 16
3. 10
4. 18
5. 140
6. 160
7. 100
8. 180
9. 4
10. 8
11. 6
12. 40
13. 80
14. 60
15. 20
16. 16
17. 40
18. 2
19. 10
20. 14
21. 5
22. 9
23. 3
24. 1
25. 6
26. 2

Activity: Toy Order Form (p. 50)

baboons: swings, 17; chimpanzees: rope ladders, 13; lions: scratching logs, 3; penguins: rubber fish, 5; snakes: color hoops, 15; prairie dogs: tubes, 9; sea lions: balls, 11; walruses: slides, 7

Practice Page #5 (p. 51)

1. 6, 13
2. 8, 17
3. 4, 9
4. 3, 7
5. 2, 5
6. 5, 11
7. 8, 17
8. 7, 15

Journal: Answers will vary.

Review Page #5 (p. 52)

1. 13
2. 15
3. 11
4. 3
5. 13
6. 9
7. 17
8. 5
9. 9
10. 7
11. 17
12. 11
13. 7
14. 15
15. 5 + 6, 6 + 5
16. 8 + 9, 9 + 8
17. 12
18. 13
19. 13
20. 120
21. 130
22. 130
23. 8
24. 9
25. 9
26. 80
27. 90
28. 90

Activity: Petting Zoo Inventory (p. 53)

pigs: + 5; rabbits: + 7; sheep: + 4; llamas: + 8; ponies: + 6; cows: + 9; donkeys: + 3; goats: + 1; ducks: + 2; geese: + 5

Practice Page #6 (p. 55)

Chart: 4, 2, 9, 7, 5, 6, 8

Journal: No, because 4 + 2 + 5 = 11. She could fit 10 on the page and she will have 1 left over.

Review Page #6 (p. 56)

Chart: 1 + 9 = 10; 2 + 8 = 10; 3 + 7 = 10; 4 + 6 = 10; 5 + 5 = 10; 6 + 4 = 10; 7 + 3 = 10; 8 + 2 = 10; 9 + 1 = 10

1. 10
2. 15
3. 14
4. 10
5. 10
6. 9
7. 10
8. 10
9. 18
10. 8
11. 17
12. 11
13. 12
14. 4
15. 13
16. 6
17. 5
18. 10
19. 10
20. 16

Activity: Special Additions (p. 59)

toucans: 9 + 1 = 10, roadrunners: 9 + 2 = 11, hummingbirds: 9 + 3 = 12, cockatoos: 9 + 4 = 13, ostriches: 9 + 5 = 14, macaws: 9 + 6 = 15, emus: 9 + 7 = 16, bald eagles: 9 + 8 = 17, penguins: 9 + 9 = 18

Practice Page #7 (p. 60)

1. 10
2. 15
3. 13
4. 16
5. 14
6. 17
7. 12
8. 11

Journal: You can just double 9 to get 18 or make ten then add 8 more to get 18.

Review Page #7 (p. 61)

1. 11
2. 12
3. 16
4. 18
5. 13
6. 14
7. 17
8. 15
9. 12
10. 13
11. 17
12. 17
13. 8
14. 9
15. 10
16. 12
17. 10
18. 16
19. 15
20. 14
21. 14
22. 7
23. 13
24. 16

Activity: Harmonious Habitats (p. 62)

Answers will vary.

Practice Page #8 (p. 63)

1. 4 + 5 = 9
2. 6 + 7 = 13
3. 7 + 3 = 10
4. 2 + 9 = 11
5. 3 + 5 = 8
6. 8 + 6 = 14

Journal: Same: addends and the sum. Different: The order of the addends.

Review Page #8 (p. 64)

Chart: 4 + 5 = 9, 8 + 7 = 15, 2 + 3 = 5, 7 + 9 = 16, 9 + 8 = 17, 7 + 6 = 13, 6 + 9 = 15, 9 + 4 = 13

1. 18
2. 13
3. 10
4. 12
5. 100
6. 100
7. 7
8. 14
9. 10
10. 60
11. 11
12. 80
13. 40
14. 11
15. 13
16. 9

Activity: Shopping List (p. 65)

carrots: 10 pounds; lettuce: 6 heads; kale: 12 heads; spinach: 8 pounds; corn: 10 ears; mangoes: 7 whole mangoes; melons: 8 whole melons; meat: 9 pounds; eggs: 11 dozen; apples: 11 cases

Practice Page #9 (p. 66)

1. 8
2. 8
3. 6
4. 12
5. 11
6. 8
7. 49
8. 31

Journal: Story problems will vary. To use the Counting On strategy, start with 16 and count ahead 2 numbers: 17, 18. You land on 18, the answer.

Review Page #9 (p. 67)

1. 9
2. 12
3. 6
4. 11
5. 8
6. 8
7. 13
8. 20
9. 22
10. 28
11. 47
12. 20
13. 28
14. 13
15. 18
16. 10
17. 17
18. 73
19. 12
20. 9
21. 7
22. 8
23. 26
24. 8
25. 10
26. 11
27. 14
28. 38

Activity: Animal Addends (p. 68)

Answers may vary but these are the most efficient choices:

12, Make 10 and then Counting On (or Counting On and then Doubles)
12, Doubles and then Counting On
16, Doubles Plus One and then Counting On
15, Special Nines and then Counting On

Practice Page #10 (p. 69)

1. 10	4. 10
2. 24	5. 18
3. 18	6. 22

Journal: Make Ten first: 7 + 3 = 10
8 + 2 = 10. Then add 6 to the two tens to
make 26.

Review Page #10 (p. 70)

1. 12	14. 9
2. 15	15. 11
3. 8	16. 16
4. 15	17. 31
5. 12	18. 16
6. 10	19. 37
7. 30	20. 17
8. 25	21. 87
9. 19	22. 30
10. 22	23. 9
11. 47	24. 13
12. 28	25. 58
13. 11	

Activity: Zoo Stamps (p. 72)

1. 8 cents	6. 15 cents
2. 5 cents	7. 9 cents
3. 5 cents	8. 19 cents
4. 12 cents	9. 22 cents
5. 16 cents	10. 35 cents

Practice Page #12 (p. 73)

1. 6	5. 4
2. 4	6. 3
3. 6	7. 26
4. 6	8. 68

Journal: The Counting Back strategy is
helpful for the 73 – 2 because it is only 2
jumps back from the original number. For
the equation 65 – 7, you need to make
7 jumps and it would not be efficient or
helpful.

Review Page #12 (p. 74)

1. 6	10. 44	19. 10
2. 4	11. 71	20. 4
3. 4	12. 16	21. 84
4. 5	13. 8	22. 6
5. 8	14. 8	23. 33
6. 5	15. 9	24. 3
7. 10	16. 7	25. 34
8. 14	17. 67	
9. 16	18. 6	

Activity: Eggsactly Related (p. 75)
Answer order will vary.

Activity: Animal Memory (p. 76)
Frog: 6 – 2 = 4, 2 + 4 = 6; Komodo dragon:
12 – 5 = 7, 7 + 5 = 12; Turtle: 9 – 6 = 3,
6 + 3 = 9; Snake: 7 – 6 = 1, 6 + 1 = 7;

Penguin: 18 – 9 = 9, 9 + 9 = 18; Fish: 10
– 8 = 2, 2 + 8 = 10; Duck: 8 – 3 = 5, 5 + 3
= 8; Ostrich: 8 – 2 = 6, 2 + 6 = 8; Lizard: 9
– 1 = 8, 1 + 8 = 9; Platypus: 14 – 8 = 6, 8 +
6 = 14; Sea Turtle: 13 – 6 = 7, 6 + 7 = 13;
Roadrunner: 11 – 7 = 4, 7 + 4 = 11

Practice Page #13 (p. 78)
Chart: 14, 12, 12, 11, 7, 9, 4, 10

Journal: Answers will vary.

Review Page #13 (p. 79)
Chart: 13 – 7 = 6, 13 – 6 = 7; 10 – 3 = 7,
10 – 7 = 3; 11 – 8 = 3, 11 – 3 = 8; 16 – 9 =
7, 16 – 7 = 9; 9 – 4 = 5, 9 – 5 = 4; 15 – 6 =
9, 15 – 9 = 6; 7 – 5 = 2, 7 – 2 = 5; 14 – 6 =
8, 14 – 8 = 6

1. 14	7. 3	13. 9
2. 6	8. 9	14. 8
3. 14	9. 8	15. 13
4. 10	10. 7	16. 5
5. 2	11. 16	17. 13
6. 7	12. 16	

Activity: Fish Shipping Form 1 (p. 82)
Chart: 36; 178; 89; 88; 374; 336; 79; 189;
179; 69

Practice Page #14 (p. 83)

1. 69	5. 69
2. 98	6. 96
3. 189	7. 489
4. 387	

Journal: There would be 7 in the holding
tank and 8 groups of ten or 80 in the main
tank.

Review Page #14 (p. 84)

1. 88	9. 68
2. 88	10. 57
3. 69	11. 72
4. 96	12. 90
5. 44	13. 199
6. 80	14. 157
7. 69	15. 999
8. 87	16. 949

Activity: Fish Shipping Form 2 (p. 85)
Chart: 50; 200; 50; 69; 303; 241; 46; 140;
171; 110

Practice Page #15 (p. 86)

1. 72	5. 85
2. 208	6. 71
3. 83	7. 206
4. 393	

Journal: If you get a number 10 or higher
when adding the ones, tens, hundreds,
. . . column then you will need to regroup.

For a sum of 9 or less you do not need to
regroup.

Review Page #15 (p. 87)

1. 98	9. 38
2. 126	10. 110
3. 83	11. 100
4. 150	12. 94
5. 120	13. 396
6. 146	14. 651
7. 129	15. 702
8. 140	16. 1,009

Activity: Fish Removal Form 1 (p. 88)
Blue Tang: 31; Kissing Fish: 111; Butterfly
Fish: 24; Sea Bass: 122; Flounder: 52

Practice Page #16 (p. 89)

1. 63	5. 17
2. 33	6. 16
3. 122	7. 41
4. 122	

Journal: Answers will vary. First you need to
subtract the ones column, 4 – 1 = 3. Then
subtract the tens place, 30 – 20 = 10. So he
ate 13 more cookies.

Review Page #16 (p. 90)

1. 22	9. 30
2. 31	10. 40
3. 30	11. 21
4. 60	12. 21
5. 21	13. 722
6. 20	14. 134
7. 12	15. 355
8. 5	16. 113

Activity: Fish Removal Form 2 (p. 91)
Clown Fish: 106; Emperor Angelfish: 34;
Barracuda: 178; Angler Fish: 7; Tuna: 286

Practice Page #17 (p. 92)

1. 15	5. 38
2. 31	6. 21
3. 127	7. 36
4. 95	

Journal: When you look at the column that
you are going to subtract if there is more on
the bottom then the top you will need to
regroup.

Review Page #17 (p. 93)

1. 42	9. 70
2. 23	10. 26
3. 29	11. 31
4. 46	12. 48
5. 49	13. 439
6. 41	14. 163
7. 50	15. 872
8. 49	16. 407

Reteaching Math: Addition & Subtraction © 2008 by Bob Krech, Scholastic Teaching Resources